Perfect Phrases for Motivating and Rewarding Employees

Perfect Phrases for Motivating and Rewarding Employees

Hundreds of Ready-to-Use Phrases to Encourage and Recognize Excellence

Harriet Diamond
Linda Eve Diamond

McGraw-Hill
New York Chicago San Francisco Lisbon
London Madrid Mexico City Milan New Delhi
San Juan Seoul Singapore Sydney Toronto

Acknowledgments

Our sincere gratitude to the senior executives, managers, supervisors, and employees in the companies that opened their doors to our training and consulting services during the past two decades and continue to welcome Diamond Associates. These span industries including pharmaceutical, healthcare, transportation, retail, banking, manufacturing, and utility, as well as government agencies. We especially appreciate the thousands of employees who attended Diamond Associates' seminars. We all learn by teaching, and whether we or one of our trainers conducted the course, no one returned without having learned about those behaviors, phrases, and actions large and small that shape a company's workforce.

Included on several chapter opening pages in Parts Two and Three are comments from people in current leadership positions. Our thanks to these motivators for sharing their insights with us: Maria Bordas, manager of strategic policy and planning, Aviation Department, The Port Authority of NY and NJ (NY); Dr. Susan Brenner, senior vice president, Bright Horizons Family Solutions (MA); Marcie Gorman, president and CEO, Weight Watchers of Palm Beach County, Inc. and president of the W.W. Franchisee Association, Inc. (FL); Roger Hillman, manager, Litigation Practice, law firm of Garvey Schubert Barer (WA); Armand Pasquini , area director of Human Resources, Starwood Hotels (DC); Denise Rounds, owner of Bellezza Salons at the Hilton, Caesars, and Bally's Park Place (NJ); and Monica Smiley, publisher of *Enterprising Women* (NC). We also are grateful to Ellen Diamond for her insights from the perspective of the motivated employee.

We are thankful to Peter Tomolonis for reading an early draft of this book and for making suggestions that strengthened it. Peter worked in management positions in the Human Resources and Aviation Departments of the Port Authority of NY and NJ for almost three decades before retiring. He has directly motivated or developed programs and/or systems to assist others in motivating and rewarding thousands of employees.

Clemente Toglia, a principal of Dominion Financial Group in Red Bank, NJ, advised us on financial options and incentives for employees. Motivation is one of Clem's strengths. Before launching his company, he was one of Diamond Associates' most dynamic trainers.

Finally, we acknowledge our editor, Donya Dickerson, who is a model of motivation, for her assistance and enthusiasm throughout this project, and Grace Freedson, our agent, for introducing us to McGraw-Hill and for her continuing energetic efforts on our behalf.

Contents

Contents

Contents

Contents

Preface

Motivation is the force that drives us all in every aspect of our lives. Without motivation, we wouldn't work, diet, exercise, pursue hobbies, or even get out of bed in the morning. In business, motivation is the seed at the center of every success. In Thomas Edison's enduring words: "Genius is one percent inspiration and ninety-nine percent perspiration." Without motivation, we would all be reduced to that one percent mindset, daydreaming through a window wondering why nothing interesting ever seems to happen.

Luckily, motivation is all around us, and most of us have natural drives toward satisfaction and success. Unfortunately, de-motivating forces and de-motivating people also surround us. Negativity is like a contagious disease (and it *is* the cause of much *dis-ease*). The good news is that a motivational mindset is also contagious, but spreading it takes more than hanging *happy* posters. In order to become a motivating force, you have to believe those inspiring slogans and breathe a positively motivating attitude.

When we first told people we were writing a book on motivational phrases, the first suggestion we were given was, "How about: 'Your money or your life'?" We had to admit that's a pretty motivating phrase! Obviously, it was said as a joke, but threats seem to have a high results ratio. Fear-based motivation of employees is easy. A manager gives orders, maybe shouts them, then goes into the office and closes the door. If you disturb the manager, you had better have a darn good reason. If you mess up, you're in *big trouble*, and everyone knows what big trouble means. Negative motivation such as threats of being fired, demoted, or otherwise losing opportunities or privileges may *seem* to work, but any gains will be offset by employees feeling less dedicated and, most likely, resentful. Fear-based, *or else–style motivation* does not develop loyal self-starters with positive attitudes.

Motivation through inspiration, open communication, and results-oriented feedback (both positive and developmental) requires more thought and sensitivity. It requires a manager to have a motivational mindset and to use motivational language. Of course, the greatest challenge is implementing those skills in times of trouble. The motivational manager is one who maintains a positive mindset even in difficult times.

Today's work environment is not as secure as that of decades ago when workers received gold watches for spending a quarter of a century with their companies (often in the same roles). Today, employees might stay in the same job but work for three different companies in the space of a few years because of mergers and acquisitions. Others move on seeking greener pastures or looking to get out before the "other shoe drops."

Employers face the challenge of motivating employees to stay, to become and remain productive in the face of internal and external changes, and to ensure ongoing customer satisfaction in an increasingly competitive arena. Retail customers, for example, can shop in brick and mortar shops (specialty, chain, outlet, new, used, or antique) or online (at brick and mortar stores' websites, strictly online businesses, private sellers at their own dot coms, or online auctions). The competition within each of those options is staggering.

We all want to know that our efforts—successful or not—are noticed and appreciated. We want to know what employers expect and that we are or are not meeting those expectations and why. "Talk to me" is frequently a silent shout of the unmotivated and disillusioned. *Perfect Phrases for Motivating and Rewarding Employees* gives those who manage or supervise others a jumpstart in thinking about how to communicate in a variety of work situations. These phrases should help those who must motivate others to integrate positive and developmental feedback into their day-to-day interactions.

The most effective motivation is self-motivation. Choosing to reach a goal for your own reasons is far more motivating than striving to meet that goal for someone else's. In this book, you will find perfect phrases, not only to motivate externally, but to help people identify those triggers that will spur them to greater achievement for their own reasons as well as yours, creating a win-win success strategy.

Who Can Use This Book?

This book is designed for anyone in any industry who wants to develop the motivational mindset and to use motivational phrases to inspire employees. It can be used by those in office, hotel, restaurant, healthcare, transportation, manufacturing, retail, and web-based business settings, as well as by those employed in educational, government, and nonprofit work environments. Further, butchers, bakers, and, yes, even candlestick makers, as long as they have employees to motivate, will find perfect phrases to suit them.

Please accept our broad use of the words *clients* and *customers*. We often refer to clients and customers interchangeably. For healthcare or hospitality-specific examples, we use *patients* or *guests*. Of course, we cannot refer to patients/guests/clients/customers for all broad examples that may apply. As you can see, if we listed every substitution, this would no longer be a handy *little* book.

Book Map

- **Part One** of this book lays the groundwork for successful motivational management. This section explores motivation and de-motivation, why motivation makes the difference, and gives you an opportunity to examine your own self-motivation and style. It encourages you to consider the importance of some fundamental characteristics of the motivational manager: be a change agent, set clear expectations, and lead by example.

- **Part Two** offers phrases for motivating employees in various situations. Many of the phrases will transfer directly to your own situation; others will give you a framework for substituting a relevant phrase or trigger an idea for addressing a particular case. For each, you will find *Motivational Mindsets* (motivation for the motivator) and *Motivational Phrases* (phrases you would say to motivate employees). The mindsets are as important as the phrases. A motivational mindset lends foundation and context to the phrases and helps you create an environment in which employees thrive. Successful managers know that the best motivation is open, honest communication.

■ **Part Three** focuses on benefits, perks, and rewards. Benefits, a critical component of any job package, may include insurance, wellness programs, retirement plans, and flextime. This section covers benefits that allow for different styles, energies, and employee needs. For instance, flexing the work schedule, if possible, is a motivator for many. The more you can tailor the job to the individual, the more appreciative and fulfilled that person feels coming to work. Perks and rewards include public recognition, gifts, and more. The "something extra" not only motivates and inspires but sends a clear message of appreciation.

Enter Here

Perfect Phrases for Motivating and Rewarding Employees is designed to help you strengthen your motivational force. Used as a reference, a guide, a companion, or jumping off point, this book offers a solid foundation for motivational managers, but the structure you build will always reflect your own vision and style. If your current style needs some tweaking, it is never too late. If some of the phrases in this book feel foreign to you, try them on. If you find yourself quick to say, "That won't work," stop to think about why you feel such resistance. Maybe it won't, but maybe it will; maybe it will with some minor changes. Put the concept in your own words; adapt it to your style.

You were motivated to pick up this book and you are motivated to motivate, inspired to inspire. So allow yourself to take some calculated risks to allow for the greatest payoffs.

Even difficult situations are opportunities to motivate or to model grace under fire. Whether you are looking for phrases for specific situations or looking for more context surrounding the mind of the motivational manager, like most self-help books, *Perfect Phrases* offers an opportunity for you to learn more about yourself. Enter here...

Part One

The Why's and Wisdom of Motivation: The Manager as Motivator

The manager plays a crucial role when it comes to motivation. In this chapter, you will explore your style and ways to establish a motivating environment. Such an environment is fostered by a motivator who sets a good example, clarifies expectations, and is flexible in the face of change. Also critical to establishing a motivational environment is the understanding that employees are individuals with varied drives, dreams, and personal goals.

Motivation is much more than a tool for energizing the demotivated; it puts an added spring in anyone's step. Managers may overlook high-potential performers who are doing more with less and doing it well. As essential as it is to help less productive employees become better, it is equally essential to help your most productive employees be their best.

Chapter 1

Why Motivate?

"If you want to build a ship, don't herd people together to collect wood and don't assign them tasks and work, but rather teach them to long for the endless immensity of the sea."

—Antoine de Saint-Exupéry

Motivation vs. De-motivation

Most people understand the benefits of motivating employees. We have all been de-motivated and felt undervalued. Those words work in tandem. As you read about motivational phrases and behaviors, you will notice a pattern of open communication and respect. Remember those who motivated you and those who had the opposite effect. Which ones made you feel like a valuable contributor?

The reasons for motivating are far more compelling than the excuses used for not motivating.

Excuses for Not Motivating

- "I, as the employer or manager, have the option of cycling people out as they fail to meet my expectations." Constant turnover not only stresses the "survivors" but also seriously impacts your bottom line.
- "No one motivated me. I motivated myself." Did you? How? Did any outside influences play a role? A worthwhile exploration, perhaps.
- "The paycheck is motivation enough." In today's economy, the paycheck alone is rarely enough to retain quality employees.
- "Each employee was hired to do the best possible job and should just do it." This is the workplace variation of, "I don't have to tell her I love her, I married her didn't I?"

This theory of *motivate yourself management* does little to promote self-motivation, which, if nurtured, is a powerful force. The first excuse costs time and money, not to mention lost customer confidence, while the last three obviously fail to take into account human nature.

Motivation includes both incentives and positive reinforcement, and it provides a reason beyond the paycheck for employees to care about the company. Employees who care about the company and its customers positively affect the company's success. Those who don't care have the opposite effect.

Reasons *for* Motivating

Motivated Employees:
- Contribute to a positive work environment.
- Affect the morale of those around them.

- Are team players.
- Are willing (if able) to go the extra mile in a crisis.
- Motivate clients and customers to return.
- Put a friendly face to your good name.
- Care about their company's image and success, and it shows.
- Are more likely to be self-starters and innovators.
- Have strong personal goals.
- Want to keep their jobs or move within the company.
- Have a healthy work ethic.
- Are committed to problem solving.
- Are good for business.

Unmotivated Employees:
- Do not attract or retain clients or customers.
- Negatively affect the morale of those around them.
- Often quit or get themselves fired at the company's expense.
- Do not care about the company's image and success, and it shows.
- Call in sick more often than satisfied employees in order to go do *anything* else (and may even *become* ill from the anxiety of going to a job where they feel unappreciated, even mistreated).
- Will "punch out" in the middle of a crisis.
- May do what is asked of them, but will rarely do more.

Great coaches know how to motivate. They know what pushes people need to start their internal engines. So, we send you forward with the words of Vince Lombardi: "The difference between a successful person and others is not a lack of strength, not a lack of knowledge, but rather a lack of will."

Chapter 2

The Wise Motivator

Example is not the main thing in influencing others; it is the only thing."

—Albert Schweitzer

Self-Motivation

How motivated are you to d   id
specific projects or tasks. A h   p
others motivated. You want h   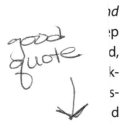 d,
and motivated employees. Wi   k-
les down to both internal and   s-
itive work environment, con   d
personal fulfillment, and leads to team success. The manager or business owner who exudes high energy and a positive outlook is motivational before ever trying. "Enthusiasm," said Ralph Waldo Emerson, "is contagious."

Your Style

Think about leaders you admire (public figures or people with or for whom you have worked) and the characteristics that describe them. What about the first manager who motivated you? The teacher who made you feel you could succeed when you doubted yourself? An inspiring family member? Pick one or two of these people and jot down some *characteristics* that define them (such as enthusiastic, energetic, calm under fire, honest, decisive, focused, flexible, careful listener). You might also include some *actions* they took that you admire (gave back to the community, found creative financing options to avoid layoffs, never shouted in the office). Underline the characteristics and actions you hold as ideals. How many describe *your* style? If you match up in all or most areas, great! If not, keep the list as a reminder of worthwhile goals.

Now look at those behaviors that detract from your effectiveness as a leader. What do you need to change? Are you typically late for meetings? Are you known as a shouter? Although everyone mutters, "That's just her style," no one appreciates it or looks forward to being on the receiving end. You are also setting a standard. Model the behavior you would like to see. Focus and build on those behaviors that define a strong leader. If it takes time, stick with it. We all have the capacity for change.

Be a Change Agent

Most people fear or feel intimidated by change; even positive change can put people off kilter. A supervisor whose feathers are easily ruffled by the winds of change will only add to the tension. On the other hand, a supervisor who expects the unexpected and doesn't get flustered is not only a calming force but also a role model for handling change.

The Why's and Wisdom of Motivation

As a manager, supervisor, foreman, or team leader, you feel the winds of change as they blow in from many directions. Corporate or company changes require your introduction to your staff or team. Often, you are in the role of salesperson convincing others of the merits of a change and the benefits to them, the company, the customers or clients, and your work product. You may have to sell a change in which you don't believe. Be honest, but supportive of the necessity for that change. The impetus for change may also come from those who report to you. You may be the one who can implement change or the only link between direct reports and decision makers. Change might also be inspired by client feedback, industry news, or, of course, your own personal insight. Your next big business idea might come from hearing someone on the street say, "Hey, I wish someone would _____ (make, write, teach, create)!" The idea is not to wait until the business is faltering or stale, but to be *always* listening, *always* looking, and *always* open to the next idea.

As a business owner, you receive motivation for change from many directions as well: change in markets, demand, customer requests, the economy, those who report to you, or your own innovation, to name a few. Positive change may come from a seemingly negative event. You lose a contract; you lose a star employee; your staple product becomes obsolete, and it feels like your darkest hours. Then, you reevaluate how you lost the contract and find ways to strengthen your presentation that put you in a better position with future prospects; your new employee has contacts and skills that make your business surge; you bring on a new product that is in greater demand than the old one had been in 20 years. When you feel blindsided by unexpected change, don't despair; think—and get your best people thinking with you.

Change is both inevitable and necessary in the process of moving forward. Not only do those in leadership roles need the ability to handle changes as they arise, but great leadership will never resist change simply because it's "not the way we do things." If you want to inspire innovators, innovate. Innovation doesn't come from rigid notions of "We *should* do this; we *should* do that, and by all means, we *shouldn't* do the other thing!" Relax. Stretch out your *shoulds*. It's good for you *and* for business to be flexible and open to new ideas.

Set Clear Expectations

The number one rule for getting what you want is to ask for it clearly. Many employees miss the mark because of misunderstandings or, as they say, managers expect them to "be mind readers." Those who report to you want to know what you expect, how you want it done, and when.

Clear expectations create a strong framework for a common purpose. Whether assigning a single task or a major project, or setting the tone for your work environment, save everyone time by stating your expectations clearly. Be clear about what behaviors are or are not acceptable. Clarify deadlines. Clear deadlines are relationship savers, face-savers, and client savers.

Clarify language. The simplest words can be misinterpreted. Don't assume that everyone's understanding of "first draft," "customer care," or "early" is the same. Clear communication goes beyond giving information. It incorporates asking questions and listening—*really* listening.

Lead by Example

Think of all the behaviors that you want your employees to demonstrate. Do you demonstrate them? For example: You want employees to be available to work overtime occasionally when deadlines are pressing, unforeseen circumstances have interfered, or things just take longer than anticipated. Are you running out the door at 5:00 or even 5:15, thanking others for carrying on the work? That won't be graciously accepted too often. Of course, if you have an obligation that prevents your staying, explain it humbly; however, don't assume that your participation—or presence—is not important. Too many late night crunches for others as you head out on time will sabotage any other efforts to motivate.

You want employees to pitch in and help others as needed. Roll up your own sleeves, too. An excellent restaurant recently closed. Shortly before this thriving start-up took a dive, the following happened: A waiter did not show up. The place was mobbed. As staff scrambled and customers waited, the owner/maitre d' maintained his role of welcoming guests and walking around and smiling and chatting. As one disgruntled diner explained, "He didn't carry out a meal or clear a table. They were clearly shorthanded. The customers waited too long for their dinners; the waiters were frazzled; and he just strolled around." By contrast, during an unusual rush at another restaurant, the manager was taking orders before the next wave of customers hit. Diners were impressed to see that they rated such care. Imagine how grateful the staff was!

Think about crises in your work environment and ways you can pitch in and help. In a crunch, no one should be above typing, collating, working a register, clearing a table, or finding a file.

Respect is another lead-by-example opportunity. You expect every employee to treat every client or customer with respect. After all, they are your organization's lifeblood. Don't badmouth the tough customers as they leave or quip about them in the presence of other clients or customers. Treating customers the way you want your employees to treat them should top your list, along with treating employees the way you want them to treat customers. Like the restaurant described above, a local shop quietly closed its doors to no one's surprise. It was typical for customers browsing in the store to hear the owner and salespeople complain about browsers who waste their time and don't buy or to be snickering about one customer in front of another. The store closed within two months.

Always remember that your behavior is setting a standard for the behavior of others. If your department has to work closely with another, prevent turf wars and interdepartmental friction by setting the tone for diplomacy. Look in your internal mirror now and then. Do you see a leader who communicates well, shows respect for others, accepts responsibility for his/her actions, shares the limelight, and demonstrates a strong work ethic? If so, these characteristics are more likely to be reflected in those who report to you. The behavior you model—whatever your intent—is the behavior others will see as the standard. "Leadership," said George Van Valkenburg, "is doing what is right when no one is watching."

Motivating Employees

You may know what motivates you, but what motivates others? Of course, not everyone fits into the same mold and not all motivational approaches work for all employees. It's easy to say someone *should* be motivated by a manager who gives out specialty chocolates, but do you know whether you're giving a box of chocolates to a diabetic, someone who is allergic to chocolate, or someone who—believe it or not—just doesn't like chocolate? Forget what you think people *should want* and find out what they *really want*. Great motivators are not self-centered. They are other-centered. They understand the difference between the employee motivated by "space to work" and the one who works best with periodic oversight. Just as everyone doesn't like chocolate, everyone doesn't like space or lack of it. Some people are most creative working alone; others are energized by a group dynamic.

Your role as motivator begins with your mindset. In Part Two of this book, you will find *Motivational Mindsets* and sample *Motivational Phrases* that support them.

Part Two

Words carry immense power. They can motivate, encourage, promise hope, and make people feel like part of something special; conversely, they can de-motivate, discourage, and make people feel alienated or taken for granted. In the wrong hands (or mouths, we should say), words can be weapons, even when that's not the intent. Some people simply believe others would be embarrassed by praise, or that a little shouting or name-calling is part of the process and that no one really takes jabs at their competence to heart. Your best bet is to assume people take words at face value and that they may be more sensitive than you think. Remember, too, that no one has ever been hurt by well-deserved, genuine praise.

So, choose your words carefully—those you use out loud, as well as those you use in your own inner dialogue. Your life, it is said, is a reflection of your thoughts. As a supervisor or business owner your work environment, too, is very much a reflection of your thoughts. Your words contribute to the experience of those around you. Everyone has off days, but if you've created a truly motivational environment, you or the employee with the off day will be supported, maybe even uplifted, instead of pulling everyone down. Positive environments give off a positive charge; the first step in motivation is creating that environment.

Chapter 3

A Positively Motivating Environment

"Life is what we make it. Always has been, always
will be."

—Grandma Moses

M otivation thrives under managers and supervisors who
create a positive atmosphere, one in which people
feel supported, valued, and respected. A motivational
work environment is charged with energy. Working in an environment without motivation is similar to slogging through mud.
You can have all of the "rah rah" meetings you want and use
positive slogans, but if you allow an employee to be harassed or
to be treated disrespectfully, your positive efforts will appear
hypocritical. Pushing through negativity to get the job done
takes a great deal more effort than being encouraged by positive language and feedback, feeling appreciated, and working
with an overall sense of team spirit.

A number of leaders describe a positive environment as one
that encourages risk and allows room for error when taking risks.
Armand Pasquini, area director of Human Resources, Starwood

Hotels, put it this way: "So many managers are concerned about zero errors or doing things by the letter that they stifle creativity and initiative. Early in my career, one manager said something to me that had a profound impact and released my creativity. Recognizing that my focus on not making mistakes was holding me back, he said, 'I dare you to make a mistake that I can't fix.' I find myself saying the same thing to those whom I manage today." Marcie Gorman, president and CEO, Weight Watchers of Palm Beach County, Inc. and president of the W.W. Franchisee Association, Inc., transferred a two-word mantra she used successfully with the nation's #1 weight loss program to any work situation: "Just stop! If you discover that you made an error, don't feel guilty, don't dwell on it, don't cover it up, don't make it any worse, just stop. Then, regroup, learn, and forge ahead."

A Positive Workplace

The Motivational Mindset

- The positively motivating environment is one in which employees feel welcome, comfortable, and appreciated.

- Start the day with a friendly greeting. Show a sincere interest in employees.

- Positive phrases can often replace negative ones. Instead of saying, "I can't stand this project," try, "This project is really challenging!" Positive words change your tone.

- *Yes* is more inspiring than *no*, even if it's a *Yes, but...* If you cannot say *yes* because of timing, say, *Yes, but not right away*. Instead of dismissing a new idea completely, is there some part of that idea to which you can say *yes*? Would you accept the idea with certain revisions? If *yes* is a possibility but not a certainty, then *maybe* is appropriate.

- Of course, *no* is a necessity, too. Without *no*, you would be doing everything for everyone, joining countless committees and crusades, and taking on responsibility for every organization that reaches out to you. *No's* can be polite and even supportive and encouraging. Most importantly, they can be critical to self- and employee-preservation.

- Champion family-friendly policies (without creating an environment in which single people are penalized with extra work and late hours to accommodate).

- Acknowledge employees' rights to life outside of work. Understand that people having made previous plans that are hard to change does not mean they don't want to contribute and would not stay late under other circumstances.

➡

- More and more family-friendly companies offer onsite daycare. The employee who knows that his/her child is in a safe, caring environment just steps away, focuses on work rather than worrying.
- Create a positive physical environment. Consider fresh paint, temperature, ergonomics, cleanliness, and lighting.
- Keep a library of motivational books that employees can borrow. Encourage people to share helpful resources that they find on their own.

Motivational Phrases

- "Good morning."
- "How are you?"
- "Yes."
- "Yes, as soon as I complete this _____ (project, phone call, letter…)." *or* "Yes, if you can help me by _____ (researching one aspect, making a few phone calls, staying a half-hour late…)."
- "Maybe. Let me see how long this _____ (report, reconciliation, inventory, phone call will take…)."
- "What a beautiful picture of your _____ (son, daughter, husband, wife…)."
- "I know you are concerned about your _____ (mother, husband, child…). Please feel comfortable calling _____ (home, the hospital, the daycare center…) a few times today to check. Let me know if you need to leave early."
- "It's going to be a challenging day. Grab your coffee and let's get started."
- "I'm glad we have such a strong crew here. We're short staffed and it's going to be a busy day."
- "I appreciate your _____ (helping Sally,

➡

20

covering for Joe, coming in early, staying late…).”

- “You’re right to be upset about what that _____ (customer, client, coworker, supervisor…) did, but what can we do to get back on track or maintain a positive focus? Is there anything we can learn from that interaction?”

- “I’m excited about this new project, and I look forward to hearing your ideas.”

- “I would like to see you leave early for your son’s soccer game, but we have a lot to get done. Can you come in an hour early tomorrow?”

- “We are now offering pre- and after-school programs as well as all-day child care. All employees who are parents are invited to attend one of the scheduled orientations.”

- “What a great day! Thanks for all of your hard work.”

Respect

The Motivational Mindset

- *Respected* is not synonymous with *feared*. You will gain more genuine respect by being other-centered, open, communicative, and friendly than you will by being autocratic. The supportive leader is no less capable of getting the job done than the feared one. In fact, your employees will be more motivated and more loyal. Fear is a shortsighted, short-term motivator with limited returns.

- Just as support staff is there to support you, you are there to support them. When a manager loses sight of the give-and-take required, support staff is more likely to give only the very minimum. Give, on the manager's part, can be anything from coaching or providing training to praise for good work.

- Be consistent with everyone. Be flexible and make exceptions, when appropriate, but not always for one person or based on favoritism. You will breed resentment for you *and* the person receiving your favors.

- Not everyone feels positive about every employee all the time. Showing respect is especially important when an employee disappoints you or pushes your buttons. Sometimes, what's in your head just shouldn't come out of your mouth. Any goodwill or show of respect you have developed will be immediately demolished by phrases such as "How stupid can you be?," "You did *what* again?," "I don't have time for this nonsense," or "For crying out loud!" Deal with problems head on, but even the most difficult situations can be handled with respect and self-control.

➥

- You won't earn respect if you don't follow through on promises. If you cannot follow through, say so, explain why, and suggest alternatives.
- Take responsibility. In some corporate cultures, it's nearly a lost art and will be highly respected.
- Admit to being wrong. You will gain more respect than you might lose by insisting you were right in the face of all reasonable evidence.
- Admit to not knowing something. You couldn't possibly know everything. No one does. Say you will find out, refer the employee to the right person to ask, or ask the employee to track down the answer.
- All employees deserve respect and common courtesy, no matter what their role in the organization. Employees must also feel respected by other employees, feel safe in the workplace, and know that all complaints are taken seriously.
- A clear message that harassment or discrimination of any kind is unacceptable creates a positive environment.

Motivational Phrases

- "Please" and "Thank you."
- "Even great ball players don't hit home runs all the time, but their fans continue to believe in them. You did your best, and I believe in you."
- "I know I promised to make time for that _____ (meeting, presentation, discussion…) on Friday, but I have to deal with a problem that just came to my attention. Can we reschedule for Monday morning? How is 10 a.m.?"
- "It's clear that we don't see eye to eye on this issue, but I respect your point of view."

➥

- "I have faith in your abilities."
- "I don't know the answer to that question. Let me find out for you."
- "Our policies are designed to protect your rights."
- "You must have been upset by that comment. I'll talk with X immediately."
- "Harassment is unacceptable." *Or any reprimand of someone who is not showing respect and any action that makes an employee (a victim of persecution or harassment) know that he or she is in a safe, respectful environment.*
- "Sexual, racial, or ethnic jokes or any comments that may compromise someone's sense of dignity have no place in this office."
- "I don't expect you to accept disrespectful behavior from anyone. I encourage you to clearly tell Lisa that she may not speak to you that way. If the problem persists, please let me know and I will speak to her."
- "I understand that you felt insulted and the customer was wrong, but you cannot talk to customers that way."
- "Have you met William? He's the _____ (writer, researcher, point person…) who makes me look so good at management meetings."
- "You were right."
- "I was wrong. I'm sorry."

The "Everyone Counts" Attitude

The Motivational Mindset

- No one is "just a…" The most demoralizing phrase in business is "just a _____ (secretary, assistant, maintenance worker, sales clerk, receptionist, order taker, store manager, foreman…)."
- If someone says, "I'm just a…" say, "You're not *just* anything! Here's why what you do is important…"
- The motivated autoworker is building a car. The unmotivated one is tightening bolts.
- People need to believe that the work they do is valuable, and it *is* or you wouldn't have hired them. Let them know how important they are to the company, the process, and the outcome.
- Employees who naturally take pride in their work will stop taking pride if they're knocked down a peg or two.
- Self-esteem is motivational and feeling valued by supervisors and coworkers strengthens self-esteem.
- Even employees with good self-esteem want to feel valued in the workplace.
- Employees making others feel small cannot be tolerated in a motivational environment.
- Some employees put themselves down. Be sure to give them specific examples of why they shouldn't.
- A manager who makes an employee feel small gets less of an employee.

Motivational Phrases

- "You're the one out front. To a customer at your register, you're the face of this company."

- "The way you deal with customer complaints adds to customer retention, and those customers are telling others about us and how well our company treated them."
- "You're not just a _____ (paralegal, research assistant, fact checker…). Your work is critical to the _____ (accuracy, success, substance…) of my work."
- "If we didn't have you proofreading, think of all of the mistakes that would have left this office on our company letterhead. You do your share to uphold our company image."
- "When you answer that phone, you're the voice of this company and the way you make people feel comfortable tells them that this company cares."
- "As the receptionist, you're the one receiving all clients and customers. In many cases, you're their first impression of our company."
- "You're not just ringing sales. The customer's interaction with you shapes that person's experience with our store and your sense of humor certainly keeps this place bright and cheerful."
- "Client relations are the very heart of this business."
- "You're not 'just a driver.' You are responsible for ensuring the safety and comfort of our _____ (customers, executives, passengers…)."
- "Packaging is a critical last link in the sales process. When customers receive damaged goods it can risk the sale and the relationship."
- "Your job is essential to everything we do. If supplies aren't stocked, everyone is scrambling. We count on you to keep things running smoothly."
- "If the shelves aren't stocked, customers will go elsewhere

➡

looking for items we have right in the back. Your efficiency affects the whole sales process."

■ "Keeping this _____ (hotel, restaurant, spa…) clean is as important as every other service we offer. If people come in and see dirty (floors, carpets, dishes…) they're likely to turn around and leave."

■ "I realize this position is a stepping stone for you. Any experience you gain here will help you in the future. In the meantime, the work you do is valuable, and we all appreciate your competence and enthusiasm."

■ "Your position is important to this company's _____ (bottom line, sales process, production, customer retention, finished product…) because _____."

The Motivational Mindset

- Excessive stress causes illness, lower morale, and a feeling of dread, in many, of coming to work. No one wants to live in a constant state of high stress.

- Your decisions, behaviors, and ability to handle stress have a direct impact over the stress of employees who report to you. Know your own stress levels and take command of your reactions. In hectic times, your state will either add to the problem or be part of the solution.

- Are you overextending your department? Are you overextending yourself, and by extension, your department? Assess what you can do to change the state of your office.

- A well placed *no* could keep you from crossing the line from a "bustling workplace" to an out-of-control environment in which frenzied mistakes and burn out are the norm. Before you say *yes*, consider the importance of the request and available resources. It's okay to say, "I'll think about it," "Let me check our workload," or "Can it wait until next week?"

- Do you praise employees for coming in horrendously sick? Would the company really have folded if they stayed home? How productive were they? What mistakes could have resulted from a groggy work state? How many work hours were lost when others caught the bug and had to stay home? If someone's that sick, recommend bed rest (and maybe some soup).

- Burning out your staff won't help you build momentum. If you own your own business and it's growing too fast,

➡

you may want to extend yourself to meet demands. (Hire one or two more people if, to satisfy you, one would have to work around the clock.) Usually, the additional financial output comes back in multiples. If that won't work for you, slow down until you're ready to consider expansion.

- Not every fire is a fire; not every tragedy is a tragedy. Being selective in emergency responses helps *real* emergencies get the immediate attention they deserve. What would happen to emergency response systems if people called 911 every time a cat was stuck in a tree or they wanted to ask a general question?

- A short break—one for fresh air, a phone call, meditation, stretching, or simply not doing anything at all, maybe even just thinking (or not thinking)—can change the tenor of a day.

- Any investment in teaching stress management techniques is worthwhile for handling both long- and short-term stresses. Fight or flight is a defense mechanism that physically geared us to react in the wild. In the office, the urge to fight or flee often leads to explosion (conflict) or implosion (self-doubt, depression, anxiety).

- Do you have a sense of humor? Do you encourage openness to humor (that doesn't target any person or group)? Laughter is a wonderful de-stressor.

Motivational Phrases

- "The scope of this proposal grows with every client conversation. Let's stop and assess what we can realistically do within our deadline."
- "I know everyone already has a packed agenda, but the XO contract is a big opportunity for us, and David needs

➡

some assistance in preparing for tomorrow's meeting. Let's figure out how we can pool our resources to pitch in."

- "Machinery does break down—usually at the worst time. Take a deep breath and explore your options for completing this project."

- "That customer was totally out of line in dumping on you like that. I appreciate your diplomacy in handling her. Why don't you take a five-minute break?"

- "You cannot control everything that happens. You *can* control how things affect you. Take three slow, deep breaths. It really does help."

- "Losing that _____ (sale, client, computer file…) must be upsetting. We've all been there. What steps are you thinking about for recovery or for moving forward?"

- "Mistakes are part of the learning process. Let's look at the lessons this situation presents."

- "I'm not blaming you for what happened. I understand what led you to make that decision. Let's address that cause and see how we can keep that same mistake from happening again to you or someone else."

- "You sound terrible! Stay home and get well."

- "You cannot control how customers speak to you but you *can* keep your stress level down by controlling your reaction."

- "Don't take a client's anger personally. Odds are the anger has nothing to do with you and is simply frustration with the situation. Stay calm and try to help. Your concern will usually turn that client's mood around."

- "We pushed hard for that deadline, but we did it! I appreciate your efforts."

- "Are you sure you want to take on that added responsibility? You already seem to be on overload. I don't want to see you burn out."

- "I know how hard you worked on this project, and it's frustrating that its success is in someone else's hands now. But you can relax knowing you did your part and, whatever the outcome, you did a great job."

- "Let's take a 10-minute break to stretch and get some fresh air."

The Motivational Mindset

- Everyone has ideas, and diverse perspectives are always useful.
- Every member of the team must be treated as equal. No one should be talked down to by a manager or team member.
- If you are creating multiple teams and have conflicting personalities among your staff, put them on separate teams. Interpersonal trials arise within any team, but you do not need to set the stage unnecessarily. Your goal is not to test their abilities to deal with one another; your goal is to create a team that will get the job done.
- The most talented member is not necessarily the best choice for team leader. Look for someone who is fair minded, has good organizational skills, and is respectful of other team members.
- No task within a team project is small or menial. All contributions are part of the end result.
- Develop a staff with a customer-centric team spirit.
- A hierarchy in which the _____ (manager, supervisor, team leader…) shoulders all responsibility and takes all credit is less likely to create buy-in and dedication among members.
- Everyone deserves credit when the team does well.
- Individuals who put in extra time and energy or act beyond the call of duty deserve individual recognition as well as being recognized as part of a successful team.

Motivational Phrases

- "I don't want anyone to feel isolated. We are all part of a team."
- "Each member of this department is valuable."
- "We are here to support each other, not judge. If someone is stuck with a problem, we need the team to pull together and offer solutions."
- "Your team has done an exceptional job."
- "Your team has done very well and your work within the team has been outstanding."
- "Your team had some issues with this project, but I appreciate your hard work and leadership."
- "Personalities always come into play in team situations, but we all have to be careful not to take things personally or to make personal criticisms. Feedback should be relevant to the team's success."
- "You are a strong group of individuals, and I predict you will gain even more strength as a team."
- "Even the most creative thinkers cannot access the level of perspective that a group of people with differing points of view can generate. I expect the outcome of your working together to be especially interesting since you are all creative thinkers on your own."
- "You are dependent on each other, so trust is important. If you have had interpersonal issues that will start you off on the wrong foot, I suggest that you address them early on."
- "The team needs to take responsibility without blaming individuals; at the same time, individuals must take responsibility if we are to learn from mistakes and strengthen the team."

- "I suggest brainstorming _____ (ideas, solutions, ways to raise money, low-cost marketing solutions…) on your own, then brainstorm as a team. You may be surprised to see how many possibilities present themselves after you think you've exhausted every avenue."

- "Strong personalities working together are bound to have disagreements, but the process of resolving those differences will open up new avenues that may not have been explored otherwise."

- "Please share your knowledge and expertise. You will not diminish your value by helping to strengthen others; in fact, management will appreciate you even more."

- "I have a great feeling about what this team can accomplish."

Productive Meetings

The Motivational Mindset

- Begin on time.
- Share and follow an agenda, and keep the discussion focused and moving forward.
- Encourage sharing ideas and strategies. Allow the group to brainstorm solutions to problems.
- Control the flow, slowing down when critical issues arise.
- Avoid putting people on the spot unless it's unavoidable. If you want someone to publicly present an idea or explain an issue, ask that person ahead of time.
- Talk about achievements and give kudos and thanks to those who have earned them.
- Talk about challenges from the perspective of seeking solutions.
- Share positive customer service reviews of the company and of individuals by name. Share negative comments, but do not name names. Speak to those employees privately.
- Discourage *groupthink*, which may be exhibited by consistent blanket agreement. A manager who encourages individuality and is comfortable with dissent can prevent perpetual groupthink.
- End on time and conclude with clear direction.

Motivational Phrases

- "Thank you all for coming. I know this meeting was called last minute, but I hit a snag and I need everyone's creative thinking on this one."
- "Our _____ (guest relations, sales initiatives, pro- ➡️

duction…) has been doing well. How can we go from good to great?"

- "Daniel and Christie, tell us how your project is going. Have you encountered any areas where you have questions or need support from the team?"

- "Sonya came to me with an interesting idea. Sonya, would you please share your idea with everyone?"

- "We recently received a lot of customer complaints about _____ (our new product, turnaround time, service wait, service quality…). I called this meeting to generate ideas about ways we can be _____ (more helpful, faster, more responsive…)."

- "We're on schedule with most of our projects, but this one seems to be lagging. Please share your ideas about what might be holding up its progress and what we can do to get it up to speed."

- "Our new website has attracted a lot of interest. The design team is to be commended. Now we need someone to take on the responsibility of tracking traffic and sales. Who can volunteer? That report will be a significant contribution to our monthly meeting."

- "We laid out a lot of new initiatives recently. Let's review how we're doing so far."

- "Our regular contributors always offer excellent suggestions. I suspect we have other good ideas at the table. I'd like everyone to have a chance to speak."

- "I would like to go back to Gordon's statement…"

- "Vi received an award from _____ for _____. Let's all give him a round of applause."

- "Gloria, as always, I appreciate your many suggestions. However we only have a half-hour for this meeting and

➥

a tight agenda. Can we go into greater detail later?"

- "Let's summarize our decisions and review who has agreed to complete what tasks by when."
- "We'll circulate a summary. Please review and react within three days of receiving it."
- "Does this time work for everyone? Good. See you next week. Thank you."

Chapter 4

Ongoing Performance Management

"Continuous effort—not strength or intelligence—is the key to unlocking our potential."

—Winston Churchill

Performance management is more than just an annual or semi-annual isolated review meeting. Performance management is a process that builds on continual feedback—both positive and developmental. The process includes setting clear expectations and goals, observing behavior, providing feedback, support, corrective action, and, at regular intervals, the performance review meeting. Ongoing performance management should communicate and reinforce the organization's mission, vision, and values. Employees need to and are entitled to know expectations, priorities, success measures, and their status in meeting these expectations.

Clearly, ongoing communication is key to a successful process. Roger Hillman, Esq., manager of the Litigation Practice of the law firm, Garvey Schubert Barer, advocates initiating ongoing dialogue: "It's not enough to say, 'My door is always open.' You have to stand up and walk through it."

Skill development is also an important part of the performance management process. Encourage employees to tap into internal or external training programs, online courses, mentoring, or on-the-job training. Don't forget to help your high-potential performers continue to grow.

Following is an actual quote: "Of course, you can't receive an 'Excellent' rating on your review. You're only a secretary and don't contribute to the company's bottom line." This quote is anonymous, for obvious reasons.

Ongoing Positive Feedback

The Motivational Mindset

- Positive feedback builds self-esteem, confidence, and goodwill.

- Think of the phrase: "Catch them doing something right," coined by Ken Blanchard in *The One Minute Manager,* to remind yourself to give the always-appreciated pat on the back.

- Kudos need no special occasion. Minor accomplishments are *still* accomplishments and *all* skills and positive behaviors add value.

- The employee who rarely excels needs the boost of an occasional "Way to go!" more than anyone. Find something to praise.

- Even your top performers need to know that you are aware of their efforts and successes. Without positive feedback, they may eventually wonder, "Why bother?" or decide to move to a more constructive environment.

- Major accomplishments deserve major praise.

- The best positive feedback is specific and goes beyond vague accolades to praise specific behaviors. *So-So Positive Feedback*: "You were great in that meeting." (That's fine to say, but add why or how.) *Useful Positive Feedback*: "Your tactfully bringing that meeting back on track saved our client relationship. I appreciate your initiative."

- Start to notice how often you give positive feedback and to whom you give it.

- Praise is positive feedback for a job well done, but positive feedback encourages the good efforts of even those who are struggling. Even if it's only a small part within the

➡

whole of an effort that has not gone well, praise the good efforts as something to build upon.

■ Praise can be given privately, publicly, in writing, online, and in letters or e-mails copied to appropriate people.

Motivational Phrases

■ "Great job!"

■ "You really have a knack for _____."

■ "I wish I could _____ as well as you."

■ "I'm so glad we have you here to _____!"

■ "I noticed the way you _____ (handled that difficult situation, encouraged someone, worked through a problem…). Good work!"

■ "I appreciate your _____ (working late, coming in early, going out of your way to make this project a success…)."

■ "I was impressed by your _____ (skills, ingenuity, commitment, desire to learn, creativity, depth of know-ledge, way of dealing with that customer complaint…)."

■ "I know you hit some snags, but that's all part of the learning process. Overall, I am impressed with the way you handled that task. Good work!"

■ "You significantly improved on my _____ (writing, suggestion, design, marketing plan…)."

■ "Would you mind sharing that idea at our next staff meeting? I think everyone could benefit from it."

■ "I know how much you've struggled with writing that report. The results are excellent—clear and concise."

■ "Your going out of your way to assist guests with directions and to answer questions contributes to the environment we want."

■ "Your changes to that _____ (recipe, method,

➡

42

program, display…) have gotten us rave reviews."
- "Thank you for taking on that job and doing it so well. I know that our clients appreciated your thoroughness and availability throughout."
- "Nicely done! Your command of crowd control during that sudden rush of customers was incredible. You remained calm and directed."

The Motivational Mindset

■ Developmental feedback may not seem motivational on the surface. However, specific, supportive developmental feedback *is* motivational. It tells each employee *specifically* what you want and why, and how to become a stronger, more valued member of the team.

■ Without developmental feedback, people think they're doing exactly what you expect of them when they're not, and they'll continue doing it, thinking they're doing a good job. They will be far less effective than they would be with a little guidance.

■ Putting the responsibility on the employee to determine the solution to his/her behavior problem motivates that employee to follow through. By dictating a solution, you can add to the problem.

■ Never say *always* and never say *never*. Employees who are told that they *never* answer the phone are likely to feel that any time they *did* answer the phone was totally unappreciated. They begin to wonder, "What's the point?" rather than continuing (or trying) to improve.

■ Don't build up a war chest of "You dids." Address problems when you see them; after resolution, let them go. Of course, if the problem is part of a pattern, it may be important to bring it up again and, in instances of serious breaches, take corrective action. Keep a record of your feedback discussions.

■ When giving developmental feedback, focus on behaviors, not judgments. *Negative or Inflammatory Feedback:* "You're not a team player." *Specific Developmental Feedback:*

➡

"When Richard was under the gun and asked you for help in preparing his presentation, you said it wasn't your job. That behavior goes against the strong team environment that benefits all of us."

- Phrases to strike from your vocabulary: "You're so dumb/stupid/incompetent." "What's wrong with you?" "You're not the sharpest tool in the shed, brightest bulb, etc." "Well that's *your* problem, isn't it?" "Shut up!" *Cursing* (in any form or context). *Shouting*.

- Explain what the consequences will be (and why) if a detrimental behavior continues.

- If a serious problem exists, describe the problem and its history. If prior warnings have been given regarding this problem, remind the employee. Inform the employee that failure to improve could result in another warning, downgrading, or termination. Document this discussion. Follow your company's progressive discipline policy.

- If a negative behavior seems out of character, say you recognize that it is and offer an opportunity to talk. You may need to recommend or require attending programs such as anger management, sexual harassment, diversity, or counseling.

Motivational Phrases

- "I have noticed that you're quick to say to coworkers, 'I'm too busy' or 'I can't help you.' We all need to support each other and to keep a positive tone. If you're too busy, you might say, 'I can look at that in an hour. I hope that's okay' Or 'I'm pushing a deadline. Will tomorrow work?' Or you could suggest someone else who might be more available."

➡

- "Snapping at coworkers is out of character for you. Do you want to talk about what's wrong?"
- "Losing your temper on the phone with that client was inappropriate. What can you do to turn this situation around and not lose your temper next time?"
- "I realize that your mother's illness hasn't allowed you the time you need for this assignment. What can I do to help you access the resources and provide the assistance that you need to complete it?"
- "Here comes the customer who nearly inspired the phrase, 'no substitutions' on our menu. Last time, she really ruffled your feathers. I know you can juggle her requests and our chef's boundaries although that is quite a challenge."
- "You do not make eye contact with or greet customers at your register. We're here to make their shopping experience pleasant. These small things do that. You'll also find that people will be friendlier to you, and you'll enjoy your work more."
- "Have you ever walked into a store and felt that you were interrupting a meeting by requesting assistance? We all have. We don't want our customers to feel that way."
- "Mary Simms is frustrated because she's left a corrected phone number with our office twice before. Would you mind crosschecking all records, and e-mail everyone who may have reason to call her? Let's prevent any of us from calling the wrong number again. Thank you."
- "I've noticed a lot of errors in your typing since you've had to cover the phones. It's hard to keep picking up the thread if you are in and out of a document. I know the extra responsibility is interfering, but please use spell-

➡️

check and proof carefully before releasing anything. Do you have any ideas for keeping your place in the face of ongoing interruptions?"

- "Your morning meetings are productive, but they routinely run into overtime. Let's review the protocol for morning meetings so you can see how a streamlined procedure might move things along more efficiently."

- "We have no place in this office for shouting or cursing. We can resolve our issues by communicating reasonably."

- "Coworkers need your support, just as you need theirs. We are not here to knock each other down; we're here to build a strong company. I know I can count on you."

- "I don't often see you smile when you greet people. You're focused on doing a good job, but a friendly greeting is important for maintaining good customer and coworker relations. Those good relations will make your job easier and more pleasant."

- "We all enjoy your friendly attitude. However, continual chatting during work adds to everyone's end-of-day pressures. We'll all be more relaxed if we save personal conversations for personal time."

- "In the office, the Internet is used for business. Please save your personal instant messages and cyber shopping for home or your breaks. Popping on for a quick look always takes more time than we realize."

The Motivational Mindset

- Communicate the process mechanics to employees.
- Schedule annual or semi-annual performance reviews and make sure to keep the appointments you've set. Nothing is more unsettling than waiting for the ever-postponed review.
- Schedule, in advance, to allow you and the employee time to prepare.
- Approach the process with a "total picture." Do not focus on the most recent events—positive *or* negative.
- Review your own notes regarding the employee's performance during this time period as well as any coaching and feedback discussions and their results.
- Determine specific changes that you want as a result of this discussion and plan open questions to focus on these changes.
- A well-planned and conducted performance review will inspire, not deflate. The goal is to help employees reach their full potential and provide guidance and support so they can.
- Ask yourself: "How will this session maintain or enhance the employee's self-esteem and self-image?" "How will this session help the employee become more effective?"
- Avoid these common pitfalls: comparing one employee to another, focusing on one aspect and generalizing, assuming the person who has your work style must be doing everything right, or attributing motives without facts.
- If your company does not have a standard form, you have a few options:

➡

A number of good books on the market include performance review forms.

Shop the web for automated or web-based performance appraisals or downloadable appraisal forms.

You can try your hand at writing a form that makes sense for your company, but don't recreate the wheel. Use resources. Reuse what works, then add or alter to make statements more relevant.

Motivational Phrases

- "Performance reviews help me keep in touch with how you are doing and what your needs are."
- "Your performance review is scheduled for Tuesday, March 3rd, at 9:00 a.m. Please bring questions or comments."
- "The review is the time to discuss your performance goals and how you are meeting them. Please come prepared to share your specific ideas about how you are doing."
- "The performance review is nothing to be nervous about. It's a benchmark that will be useful to both of us."
- "Think about contributions you've made of which I might not be aware. I'll want to learn about them at the meeting."
- "Don't be afraid to toot your own horn."
- "Salary increases are/are not directly tied to performance review ratings."
- "Think about steps you'll want to take for your personal improvement plan. Are there courses you might want to attend or projects to work on that will help you stretch your skills?"
- "Look back at your previous review so you are aware of improvements you've made and ways you have met your goals."

➡

- "Think about ways you exceeded the expectations we set last time."
- "I know this is a busy time for everyone, but these performance review meetings are essential. Your direct reports deserve your input."
- "John, when writing reviews, remember that the form is a guide. By following it, you maintain objectivity and review everyone according to the same guidelines."
- "I know reviewing others' performance is new to you. I suggest that you avoid using labels, such as 'uncooperative.' Focus on specific behaviors, for example: "Your refusal to _____ (greet a customer arriving to meet someone else, check e-mails regularly, turn your cell phone on…) is bad for business and impedes team success."
- "Think about action words when giving feedback. Whether describing what the employee does well or pointing out areas for improvement, action words give specific, meaningful feedback. For example: 'You prevented a major panic with your decisive action during the blackout.' or 'When you interrupt others during meetings, we lose time, and often, the point being made.'"
- "Be prepared to tell me how organizational policies, senior management, or I may have helped you attain your goals or prevented you from achieving them."

The Performance Review Meeting

The Motivational Mindset

- By the time the employee and employer sit down for "the talk," there should be no surprises. This meeting should be part of an ongoing dialogue in a workplace with clear communication and feedback; the employee should have a fairly good sense of what issues might arise.

- Do not allow interruptions. Your employee is counting on your feedback and undivided attention.

- Focus on specific behaviors rather than generalizations. Descriptive words and phrases such as *exceptional*, *nice job*, and *needs improvement* are fine for summing up, but do not tell the story. Identify specific actions and give details.

- Do not paraphrase general statements on the form. Use specific examples.

- Your comments should reflect employees' work in relation to their job descriptions. Filter out feelings and focus on actions. Discuss strengths and developmental needs in key performance areas. Reference objectives and previous action plans. Focus on job-related behavior and performance expectations.

- Developmental feedback is more effective when it involves the problem's causes and corrections, its effect on others within the workplace, and, if applicable, its impact on company goals, image, or client/customer relations.

- Seek to identify areas for new skill development and/or increased responsibility. Help your high-potential performers reach greater goals.

- Jointly develop an action plan with the employee and

➡

schedule interim follow-up meetings. *Follow-up is critical.* Revise goals if necessary.

- Employees should leave the performance review meeting with your comments in writing.
- Conclude on a positive note and express your interest in the employee's success. Schedule a follow-up meeting to review progress toward developmental and growth decisions.

Motivational Phrases
General

- "Are you pleased with your overall performance? Why? Why not?"
- "What would you like to change? Why? How?"
- "What changes would you like to see—in the organization, department, division, yourself—that would help you do your job? How would you suggest implementing these changes?"
- "Can you think of anything specific that I've done that helped or hindered your performance?"
- "I know you have been working to make changes we discussed in the last meeting. Are you having any problems with that?"
- "I noticed that you are implementing those changes we talked about. Keep up the good work."
- "Do you have any concerns?"
- "Do you have any suggestions?"
- "How would you feel about taking on more responsibility?"
- "I would like you to develop an action plan based on the goals we identified in the meeting. Let's review it next week."

➡

- "I understand I've given you a lot to think about in terms of choosing a direction. Let's schedule a follow-up meeting so you can take some time to consider your options."

- "I have confidence in your ability to initiate the changes we discussed. Please let me know if you have any problems and let's review your progress next month."

- "I'm very pleased with your improvement since our last discussion. I hope you are, too."

- "Once you start _____ (reworking that system, using some of the customer service skills we discussed, working on the new project team, revising your schedule…), let's meet to review progress. Put it down for two weeks from today."

- "Is there anything else you would like to discuss with me?"

Addressing Concerns

For more phrases that address concerns, refer to the earlier section in this chapter titled: "Ongoing Developmental Feedback."

- "You often seem frustrated. You start to say something and back off. I value you and your work. Let's talk about what's been bothering you."

- "Help me understand why you want a transfer. You're our top performer. Clients love you; colleagues respect you. I don't want to lose you. What led to this decision?"

- "We have all been on overload, but when you don't keep up it adds to everyone else's burden. Last week, as you know, we almost lost one of your clients who was frustrated with continual delays. What can we do to remedy this situation?"

- "Sometimes, you seem to blaze ahead without following

directions. I appreciate your initiative, but it's important that our team members work together and follow some proven courses."

- "I know that this process is confusing. Mastering it is essential to your job. What aids or tools will help you?"

- "When you come in late, others have to interrupt their work to cover for you. What can you do to get here on time?"

- "According to the action plan we created in the last meeting, you were going to _____. I noticed that you haven't begun. What is getting in the way?"

- "We have talked about what the problems are. What solutions do you see? How would you go about moving forward from here?"

- "I have noticed that you sound abrupt on the telephone. Are you aware of that?"

- "We have received a number of complaints from people who describe you as 'rude.' I'm sorry to say I don't have specifics. Are you aware of the actions or tone of voice that would lead people to say that? What are they? How do you think you could modify your _____ (tone, actions, behaviors...) to rectify this problem?"

- "You haven't been transitioning into your new role. I know you don't feel fully confident in this role yet, but I need the job done. I'm here to support you and I believe you can do it. Are you with me? Do you have reservations that I should know about?"

- "Do you realize there will be serious consequences if you continue telling racial jokes in the office? Let's review the company's definition of offensive language and the consequences for using it."

- "When you lose a sale, I can hear you shouting all the

➡

way in here! You know it's a numbers game. You just have to move on. Shouting affects everyone's morale. Please find another outlet for this frustration."

- "I appreciate your acceptance of some strong developmental feedback. Please know that my role is to help you succeed."
- "We covered a number of rough spots, but I want to stress that, overall, your work has improved significantly."

Praise

For more phrases of praise, refer to the earlier section in this chapter titled: "Ongoing Positive Feedback."

- "You've initiated three new projects during the past two quarters. That's impressive. What do you have in mind going forward?"
- "I appreciate your frankness when directions aren't clear. You save us all a lot of time."
- "You have gone above and beyond on every assignment. Your commitment to following through despite the time drain has helped not only our department, but also the entire company."
- "Your ability to jump in with creative solutions has saved a lot of time and money. I've shared that with upper management."
- "Your work is exceptional. You are detail oriented yet don't get bogged down in minutia. You continually exceed expectations."
- "You are not stopped in your tracks by problems; you create solutions."
- "I am impressed by your initiation of new projects."
- "I appreciate your eagerness to assist coworkers and to

➡

pitch in without being asked."

- "Since our discussion several months ago, I notice that you are more patient with the service department. That helps us keep things running smoothly. Thanks."
- "You are a clear communicator and I appreciate that you are quick to request explanations when I'm not as clear as I could be."
- "You have shown tremendous improvement in your ability to juggle multiple tasks. Keep up the good work!"
- "Your positive attitude is inspiring to those around you. Keep smiling!"
- "I believe that you're ready for more responsibility. How would you feel about being the team leader on our upcoming project?"
- "I just received another customer letter praising your problem-solving initiative. This customer was very appreciative that when she had to speak to someone else you handed her off personally and then went out of your way to follow up. I'm proud to have you on our team. Here is a copy of the letter."
- "I frequently pass by when you are speaking with a customer and overhear how service-oriented you are. Your keeping a friendly demeanor even under the most difficult circumstances is impressive."

Employee Goals and Growth

The Motivational Mindset

■ Understand that skill development is a worthwhile investment of time and money, and plan for it. Skill development has a variety of approaches: classroom training, computer-based training, on-the-job training, cross training, mentoring, shadowing, and jumping in with both feet. Varied methods are best suited to different employees and different skill sets.

■ When setting goals with employees, look beyond today or this year. Where does this employee want to go within the organization? How can he/she get there?

■ Goals set *with* employees are more effective than goals set *for* employees. Use the performance appraisal process as an opportunity to help employees create development plans. Establish a clear method for tracking progress.

■ Employee performance goals should be specific and should support departmental and company goals.

■ Some people want to climb as high as possible; some people are happy closer to the ground and just want to feel secure in their jobs, do good work, and go home worry free. All personality types and levels of aspiration offer value and need to feel supported in their individual goals.

■ Someone who is resistant to moving up should not be pushed because someone else believes his/her 'talents are wasted.' Express your appreciation and admiration of the employee's performance and abilities. You may (or may not) inspire that person to new heights. Praise is motivating, but an employee also needs to believe that his/her work is important and treating a job as "menial" is demoralizing.

➡

- Both fears of success and fears of failure can often be overcome in a supportive atmosphere.
- Help employees look at the next step on the career path. Though a part of us may want to selfishly hold people in place when they are doing their jobs especially well, we all know that focusing on what's best for the employee is ultimately best for everyone.
- Find out the employee's dreams. If you have or can create a position that aligns in some way with someone's dreams, there is no greater motivator and no limit to the potential for success.
- Make availability and benchmarks for promotions clear. If true potential is ahead, use the news to inspire, but if the chances are marginal don't try to inspire by building false hopes. An employee who feels he or she was led around by a fake carrot will be thoroughly de-motivated.

Motivational Phrases

- "What do you (as an individual) or we (as a department, team, or company) want to achieve? When do we want to achieve this goal? How can we achieve this goal?"
- "What goals can you set for yourself that support our department and company goals?"
- "Where do you want to go within the organization? What specific objectives and actions will help you achieve those goals? What support will you need from me? From others?"
- "Please develop a realistic timeline that we can review."
- "What skills do you have to reach the goals you've set? What training and/or support do you need?"
- "How can you help others reach mutual goals while staying on track and on purpose?"

➡

- "You have moved up rather quickly with glowing recommendations along the way. What career path do you envision?"
- "Your strong accounting background led you to finance, but your people skills are outstanding. Have you considered transferring to human resources?"
- "Where do you see yourself in five years? Ten years?"
- "You have a natural talent for ____. Have you considered honing that skill?"
- "If you learn to ____, you are in a stronger position to get a promotion."
- "Not many people in this department know how to ____. It would be a valuable skill for you to develop."
- "Times are changing and it's important for someone in your position to know how to ____. If you add this to your already strong skill set, you will further your opportunities for advancement."
- "You clearly have command of the technical aspects of the job. With improved writing skills, you could be eligible for a promotion."
- "I couldn't be more pleased with your job performance. As you can see, you've exceeded expectations in every area. What can I do to ensure that we continue to challenge you?"

Chapter 5

Modeling and Encouraging Communication Skills

"He who has a why can endure any how."

—Friedrich Nietzsche

C ommunication skills, both face-to-face and via technology, are critical to the success of any business. Ironically, in many cases, the advance of technology has increased the importance of people skills. With so many modes of communication, each of us needs to be the central pilot, the human at the hub, following up. Did the message get through? Was it comprehensible? Is this a situation that requires a human voice or presence? People who work together have differing styles, expectations, and temperaments and must understand each other explicitly to get the job done.

In 1967, Marshall McLuhan coined the phrase:"the medium is the message," emphasizing that the *how* impacts the *what*. Today, more than ever, with so many media at our disposal and real and perceived time crunches and emergencies pulling at us, choosing the medium that suits both the message and the audience, making the *clear communication choice*, is more important than ever.

The Motivational Mindset

- Think about the consequences of poor communication: mistakes; misinformation; lack of commitment; untapped potential; failure to implement change; and lost time, money, and resources.
- Be question friendly. Some people surround themselves with invisible walls that say, 'Do not disturb.' These discourage questions that, if answered, provide timesaving clarification.
- Understand that everyone doesn't process information the same way. Some people respond better to verbal instructions or information, others to written, and still others may need a hands-on demonstration. Communication styles may include paraphrasing, using examples, empathizing, or reflecting.
- Be clear about what you want and be appreciative when you get it.
- Explain new tasks clearly, step by step, demonstrating (if appropriate) and stopping along the way to ensure comprehension. Complex instructions may be best written out as well as explained. You may want to write out key points or ask the employee to take notes. If the instruction will be repeated, the document will become a handy tool for training or reference.
- Clarify deadlines and be specific. How complete do you want the task by that deadline? Do you want a status report before the final deadline? When asking someone to work overtime, be specific about times and dates.
- Everyone processes information in the framework of

➡

their own priorities unless given clear expectations and clear timeframes.

■ Involve people in the big picture. The more information you share, the easier it is for each person to succeed at his or her part of the whole.

■ Do not use jargon with anyone who is new in the industry or not in your industry. Encourage employees to do the same.

■ Actively seek feedback on your own performance. Liberally use the phrase, "Tell me more." Ask for clarification on points that seem unclear or unfounded. Carefully evaluate the accuracy and potential value of what you hear.

Motivational Phrases

■ "Our internal deadline is February 24 to allow us time to incorporate input from other departments and have a final review. Our goal is to send out the completed package by March 8."

■ "We get so used to using these words every day that we forget which are jargon. I heard you telling a customer about (some jargon phrase) and want to remind you that customers may feel intimidated by terms they don't know. What would be a customer-friendly way to say it?"

■ "What problems are you having with the new _____ (computer, checkout, registration, inventory…) system? How do you think we can address them?"

■ "How can we revise signage to clarify directions and limit travelers' frustration?"

■ "I'm so glad you spotted that woman's briefcase under the table. You saved her a great deal of trouble and reinforced our reputation of caring for customers."

➡

- "I'll be on vacation next week, so if you want my input, please get to me by Thursday."
- "Let me show you how that works."
- "I don't want to waste your time. Why not give me a brief outline or summary before you dive into writing that report."
- "Your dedication is admirable; however, your safety comes first. Please stay where you are until the weather advisory lifts the travel warning."
- "I had no idea how that additional responsibility impacted on your current workload. Let's review some options. First, what would you suggest?
- "I apologize for transposing that phone number. You must have been going crazy."
- "Thank you for bringing that problem to my attention. It does need to be addressed immediately. I'll let senior management know—and tell them that you picked it up. Nice work."
- "Let's not take anything for granted. I know you should have no problem making the arrangements we discussed, but please call or e-mail me to confirm that all scheduling details are completed."
- "Check online for step-by-step procedures. It's a lot to remember until you are completely familiar with each process."
- "I know you're pushing a deadline, but I do have to explain this to you before I leave. Please take a moment out to focus on this."

Listening for Clear Communication

The Motivational Mindset

- Show that you are listening: Make eye contact, respond, and focus on the person speaking to you.
- Ask open questions. Open questions encourage more than one-word responses. They typically start with: *what, where, how, why*, or phrases such as *tell me*, or *please explain*.
- Summarize to be certain you understand and/or are understood.
- Make clarification a way of life. Ask employees to repeat important information to you and do the same for them.
- Identify people who have good ideas but may be shy about expressing them. Encourage them to share.
- Do not interrupt, complete others' sentences, or jump to conclusions.
- Use open, attentive body language. Leaning forward, making eye contact, and keeping your arms uncrossed are all expressions of open body language.
- When people start talking to you at times when you cannot focus or listen, it is important to express that you're busy but interested and to suggest a time (or timeframe) when you can listen.
- Don't assume someone heard you just because you muttered something as you walked by while that person was otherwise engaged. Make eye contact and, if necessary, schedule a better time to talk.
- Tone of voice, word choice, and body language are all-important cues that may easily be misinterpreted. Beware of jumping to conclusions regarding these listening cues. When in doubt, ask.

➡️

Motivational Phrases

- "Let's talk in here, where we won't be interrupted. I know you've been trying to catch up with me."
- "If I understand you correctly, what you're saying is _____."
- "You've made a lot of interesting points. I'd like to summarize to be certain I understand."
- "I'm sorry if I misunderstood you. Let's see where we can go from here."
- "Let's all allow each other to share ideas without comment or criticism. Later, we'll evaluate more carefully, but I'd like everyone to feel free to let ideas flow."
- "How would that work?"
- "Why do you prefer that method?"
- "Please explain your thinking on that."
- "I'm sorry I don't have time to give you my full attention right now. Can we talk later this afternoon?" (If possible, schedule a time.)
- "You sounded upset when I called this morning. Did I misread you or is something wrong?"
- "I just blurted out this meeting information, but I see that you're focused on something else. Since I'm running out and won't be available, please jot it down so I know you have it."
- "That's a great idea, but I'm not sure it's right for us at this time because _____. Can the plan be tweaked to meet our needs more precisely?
- "I like that idea. Tell me more."
- "That's an interesting idea. Let's explore it at our next meeting."
- "I put my phone on voice mail so we can talk without interruption."

Clear Communication Choices

The Motivational Mindset

- All communication choices are not equal. Use the right medium for your message. For example, a message e-mailed at 3:00 p.m. regarding a 5:00 p.m. meeting or e-mailed late in the day regarding an 8 a.m. meeting, can easily be missed. Don't rely exclusively on e-mail for time-sensitive issues.

- Some people get hundreds of e-mails each day and just can't wade through—or may be out of the office or in meetings all day. If a message is critical, try e-mail and voice mail—or, better yet, track someone down in person if possible.

- Not everyone has the same comfort level with technology. Know your audience.

- Never assume your whole message got through while a cell phone was cutting out.

- Create short, clear voice mail messages for those calling you and leave short, clear voice mail messages when calling others.

- Leaving key information such as what you need to know and by when, your availability, and your contact information, eliminates or greatly reduces phone tag.

- Use specific subject lines in e-mails.

- Don't write mystery e-mails where the most important point is buried in the middle or saved for the end. Write the most important information up front.

- Sometimes, instead of instant messaging, e-mailing, calling, or enabling your video conferencing equipment, you might just walk down the hall and talk face to face. ➡

- Your face and body language are communication media, too. Do they fight with your message? Be aware of the visual cues you give.

Motivational Phrases

- "If you cannot reach someone through text messaging, try another method. You might be text messaging a person who doesn't use that feature. You might even be sending to a phone that does not record text messages at all."
- "I know you're discouraged by not getting a callback, and I know you said you called all day yesterday, but you also said you didn't leave a message. It's often hard to catch people, but they do check in. You'll save yourself time and frustration by leaving specific messages."
- "If your e-mails are not getting a response, try another method. Servers go down, e-mail programs can have glitches, and your name could accidentally be set to fall into the junk file. Make a call and when you connect with a live person, confirm that you have the right address and explain your problems getting through."
- "Communicating with that department is beyond frustrating. I admire your patience."
- "If you cannot be there to join us for the meeting, can you be there via phone or video conferencing?"
- "E-mail is not always my top priority, and I may not get to it the day it is sent. Please mark all urgent requests 'time sensitive' in the subject line."
- "Instant messaging does not mean the recipient is available to respond instantly."
- "Don't include anything in an e-mail that you wouldn't want to see on a billboard."

- "Don't assume everyone knows e-mail and instant messaging abbreviations."
- "Even if you don't have all of the information yet, please leave me a message filling me in as much as you can before 2:00 p.m. That will be my last chance to check in today."
- "If a message is urgent or has to be returned ASAP, I need to be told about it the minute I come in. If you are stepping out, please leave a message on my _____ (door, desk, chair, voice mail, e-mail…)."
- "Thank you so much for thinking to send the contracts by overnight mail. I hadn't thought of that and would have had a real problem if you didn't."
- "Specific e-mail subject lines are helpful: *Thursday's Meeting Agenda; Friday's 10:00 a.m. phone conference rescheduled; Thanks to those who helped with the March event; New Healthcare Policy; This Month's Contest; Company All Stars; Kudos.*"
- "Spell-check is not a mindless activity. Read the choices. *Always* spell-check and *never* rely on spelling or grammar checks without engaging your own bank of knowledge."
- "I really do like your suggestion. I've been told I have 'that face.' Don't let my expression throw you. Your idea is superb."

Chapter 6

Motivating Critical Skills

"Whatever you are, be a good one." —Abraham Lincoln

Whatever your field, certain life skills translate to good business practices. Some of these come naturally to people and others are cultivated with a little guidance and a good role model or two. Creativity, initiative, critical thinking skills, and a flexible mindset keep people thinking, contributing, and moving the company forward. Time management and organizational skills keep business, business relationships, and workflow running smoothly. Presentation skills to large and small audiences enhance information sharing. The motivational manager gently encourages building or honing these critical skills.

Developing skills requires time and effort—yours and your employees'. When that investment seems unreasonable, think of Thomas Jefferson's words:"I am a great believer in luck, and I find the harder I work, the more I have of it."

Creativity

The Motivational Mindset

- Creativity may require quiet time to think. Don't always expect a creative answer on the spot.
- People are often more creative than they realize. Giving people a chance to access their creativity will often boost self-esteem.
- Encourage the search for new solutions to persistent problems.
- If employees have creative interests outside of work, tapping into the same skills in the office might spark their creative spirits. Before you hire a company to design your brochure cover, consider the talents in your office.
- Consider a monthly (or quarterly) creativity caucus to encourage and hear employee ideas.
- Encourage brainstorming, allowing as many ideas as possible to come to the surface for consideration. The #1 rule of brainstorming: All ideas are welcome and nothing is ridiculed or put down. No ideas are wrong.
- Compliment creativity when you see it.
- When is the last time you looked through your staff's resumes? Are you overlooking skills and talents that didn't apply two or three years ago but would help you and give your employee an opportunity?
- Stark walls, fluorescent lights, and unadorned cubicles don't inspire creativity.
- Have a library available for employees that includes brief meditations or relaxation techniques. Used on breaks, these can lead to a refreshed, creative mindset.

Motivational Phrases

- "Do you have a suggestion for a new _____ (product, initiative, promotion…)?"
- "In what kind of environment do you do your most creative thinking?"
- "Take your mind off the issue for a while (perhaps over lunch). Sometimes creativity flows as soon as you stop consciously searching."
- "Why did you seem hesitant about this plan? I value your opinion and would like to know your thoughts on it. Would you mind sharing?"
- "Choose a partner to brainstorm solutions. Even wild ideas are allowed here. Whichever team gets the longest list (with no repetitions) wins a free lunch (or some small token reward)."
- "I imagine you'll find a creative solution."
- "I need some creative juices on this project. Can I have your input?"
- "How many new approaches can you come up with for dealing with this issue?"
- "What thoughts do you have on how we can turn this problem into an opportunity?"
- "We need your creative sparks in tomorrow's meeting."
- "What is your instinct on this? You have great intuition."
- "Can you find a new angle for tackling this issue?"
- "How would you approach a new client about our product line?"
- "We've used the same format for our company awards program for five years. The planning committee is requesting suggestions for changes."

➡

- "We're having a contest to rename the newsletter. The employee who submits the selected title wins a $100 gift certificate."

Initiative

The Motivational Mindset

- Initiative is not always moving *up*. Initiative can also mean stepping in to help a team member, *any* team member in need. In a crisis, everyone pitches in—including the manager. If cashiers, customer service reps, or waiters are on overload, it hurts your customers and doesn't look good for anyone. If your administrative assistant can't meet your deadline, it's your problem, too.

- Intrapreneurship has become a watchword in successful companies. The concept brings the fire and passion of the entrepreneur to employees in larger work environments. Create a sense of ownership among employees for your department's or company's success and the intrapreneurial spirit will motivate.

- Two major initiative roadblocks are indifference and negative reinforcement.

- Showing appreciation and respect for the employee who attempts to chart new ground—whether or not successful—encourages that employee and others to think outside the box.

- Employees who are encouraged to take initiative and who can see the results of their initiative in action are more likely to be motivated and take interest in the company's success.

- Forget the old adage: "If you want something done right, you have to do it yourself." Remember, instead, this new adage: "If you want something done right, delegate to the right person."

- Delegation is not dumping. Delegate to the right person;

then be available to answer questions and provide support and guidance.

- Delegate the responsibilities that will keep business running smoothly. Do not foster an environment where no one takes initiative and, for example, supplies run out causing rush, panic, or complaints. Little things, even supplies, mean a lot.
- Time invested in explaining, demonstrating, and answering questions will pay off later, when an employee has the confidence and competence to take over the role.
- By offering small windows for big thinking, employers encourage staff to reach beyond their grasp.

Motivational Phrases

- "I need someone skilled to take over this assignment. I will be here to support and train you. Would you be comfortable with the added responsibility?"
- "How are you doing on that project? I knew you would be able to run with it on your own."
- "Please check in with me as you take on your new responsibilities. I have to approve decisions during this learning phase, but I know you will be quick to pick this up and will do an excellent job."
- "Tell me how you would improve nurse-to-patient response time. You seem to be able to be in three places at once."
- "I am confident in your abilities, but feel free to ask questions anytime."
- "I'm always open to new ideas. Can you think of another approach for _____ (guest check-out, patient intake, client follow-up, work order processing…)?"

➡

- "What a fantastic idea! I'm 100 percent behind you. How can I support you?"
- "What are your ideas for solving this problem (or resolving this issue)?"
- "I have been working closely with management on reviewing our strategic plan for the next five years. I'd like to share some ideas with you and get your opinion. You're really in touch with day-to-day operations."
- "You know that we all believed that the new approach you initiated would be successful and we all share your disappointment. Try those few changes that we talked about in the meeting. Your creativity moved us forward a few steps. Your next try will help us leap ahead."
- "Our new guest relations handbook is almost ready for press. You have made excellent editing suggestions on other projects. Would you mind reviewing this?"
- "You have such great ideas, but you seem hesitant to share them. I think it would be to everyone's benefit if you could become confident about how much you have to offer."
- "You know this project inside out. My travel schedule is interfering with my role as project manager. I'd like you to take over."
- "Thanks for taking the initiative in putting passengers for the 10:15 a.m. flight in front of that incredibly long line."
- "I'll be out of the country next month. I'm confident having you present our recent initiatives at the interdepartmental meeting. Let's get together so I can explain how I typically do that."
- "You don't even have to run _____ (the changes, your ideas, your edits, the proposal...) by me. Everything you do is so on target."

Critical Thinking

The Motivational Mindset

- Critical thinking is a search for reason through a problem-solving process.
- Critical thinkers don't blindly believe everything or nothing. They see full spectrums of colors and shades, not just black and white.
- Skepticism is not necessarily negative. Healthy skepticism raises necessary questions.
- Brainstorming can continue even after you think you've hit upon the best idea. It may only be the best idea *yet*. You also may need backup plans.
- Monday morning quarterbacking should not be played as a form of regret, but as a catalyst for growth. It can be helpful to replay an incident that did not go well in order to prepare for successful future outcomes.
- Avoid jumping to simple cause and effect conclusions. For example, Bob spilled his coffee during the presentation. The client chose to contract with a competitor. Of all possible reasons for a client to choose a competitor, don't decide it was because Bob spilled his coffee.
- Encourage employees to consider other points of view, even those that sound the most outrageous.
- Look at prior experiences and consider their relevance to the current situation.
- Use and teach a simple problem-solving strategy:
  1. Identify the problem.
  2. Analyze the problem and consider possible causes.
  3. Generate possible solutions and select one.

➡

4. Implement the solution.

5. Follow up by evaluating the solution.

■ Conduct problem-solving sessions that allow everyone to participate. Allow for additional questions and creativity to broaden the experience.

Motivational Phrases

■ "How can we define this problem? What are possible causes of this problem?"
■ "What do we know from prior experience? How relevant is that prior experience to this situation?"
■ "How many possible solutions can we find? Which solution or solutions will help us achieve our desired result?"
■ "How should we prioritize solutions?"
■ "Which solutions address the cause?"
■ "Is it necessary for our solution to address the cause or is this clearly a one-time issue?"
■ "How will we implement this solution?"
■ "What process will measure the solution's success or rate its effectiveness?"
■ "What new ideas can we generate?"
■ "What possible outcomes can we imagine?"
■ "It's not important right now who forgot to confirm the hotel. What is important is how we relocate a conference of 500 people in three weeks."
■ "We're facing a difficult challenge—satisfying customers, stockholders, and regulatory agencies. Let's review common stakeholder requirements and start with those."
■ "That incident was an embarrassment to all of us. Let's explore what happened so we won't duplicate it."

➡

- "Statistics, intuition, numbers, past experience, and logic are all useful tools, but relying solely on any one of them can be a mistake."
- "Never underestimate your gut instinct. Factor it in."

Flexibility

The Motivational Mindset

- Change is life; it is the natural state of all things. A work environment that does not change stagnates.
- Complaining about change sets a counterproductive tone. Rather, determine ways to work with the change.
- Embrace change enthusiastically, and encourage others to recognize inherent opportunities.
- Fear of change is a learned response. Even learned responses can be changed. Model the positive response.
- Every time a new employee joins a company or a department, the dynamic changes slightly. The flexible leader is in tune with the shift and able to help it maintain a positive direction.
- Being flexible means remaining open to suggestions and willing to change your plan or direction if change is best—whether or not it's comfortable.
- Change, even positive change, can be a major cause of stress for many people. Our reactions to change, not the change, cause us stress. Be open to new ideas and approaches. Encourage that openness in others.
- Stressing out or stewing over a problem does not bring about change. Explore options and be proactive.
- Don't rush to judgment, good or bad; evaluate the situation and consider possible courses of action. We have all experienced so-called *blessings in disguise*.
- Once a policy change is in place and you know the time for questioning it is over, help those who report to you accept it and move on.

➡

Motivational Phrases

- "I understand that change can be stressful, but this reorganization will ultimately be positive."
- "New technology can be daunting, but we have to stay current. Group training is available every morning at 7:30 a.m. and individual training is available upon request."
- "These are exciting times for the company, and we know that you are all behind our success. Opening a new store pulls resources from existing ones. Please bear with us during this phase."
- "The new office will be different, but we can look forward to _____ (more windows, being downtown, having a conference room…)."
- "The new branch will be a place for expanded opportunities."
- "The new management does things differently. You may like some of their methods and not others, but we ask that you reserve judgment during the transition."
- "I know this is not how we've done it in the past, but let's consider whether it's the best method for the future."
- "What benefits can you see from this change?"
- "I like your new idea. We have never tried this before, so we have many possible outcomes. Let's run a few scenarios to see how it might play out."
- "This is not working out as we had planned, but the results are interesting; let's stay the course. You never know what you may discover. The inventors of post-its were trying to make glue."
- "The only constant is change. If we can be comfortable with change and expect the unexpected, we won't feel thrown 'off course' when it comes."

➡

- "What computer upgrades would make this project run more smoothly?"
- "Let's pause to assess our progress. Are we on track? Is 'on track' still where we want to be or should we consider a new direction?"
- "I'm very comfortable with the current progress, but your suggestion is interesting. Let's try it for one quarter."
- "I realize that the promotion you're considering is a major step, but I believe you have the qualities to succeed at that level. Let's talk about what your new responsibilities would be."

Time Management

The Motivational Mindset

■ Time is money—to you, your company, your clients, and your employees.

■ Compressed time, poorly managed time, and not enough time lead to errors, lost opportunities, and stress.

■ Increased media at increased speed, such as e-mail and cell phones, have created a general sense of urgency in the workplace (and beyond). Most people believe they do not have enough time to do their jobs and meet others' expectations. Control the frenzy.

■ Planning saves time—yours and others'. Plan and help others plan to achieve long- and short-term goals and, sometimes, to just get through the day.

■ Time management tools aren't in everyone's toolbox. Don't assume that all employees know how to plan. Offer guidance, seminars, and resources.

■ Help employees anticipate the unexpected. Establish a mindset where the unexpected won't have the power to wreak havoc.

■ Controlling interruptions is key to time management. Respect others' uninterrupted time and request your own.

■ Setting and synchronizing priorities is essential to good time management.

■ Understand whose crisis is your crisis.

■ Help supervisors who report to you learn to delegate appropriately. Delegating is selecting the right person for the right job, not pushing unwanted tasks on others.

➡

Motivational Phrases

- "I know that recent layoffs have increased everyone's work load. Think about these questions as you review those tasks that you now face: Is this necessary? Can it be consolidated? Can it be eliminated? Can it be delegated?"

- "I know that time tracking seems like yet another job, but it *does* help you evaluate how you spend your time. We're only doing this for one week."

- "When you are focused on typing a document, I hate to interrupt. Sometimes, like now, I just have no choice."

- "I appreciate your covering Sam's phone while he's at the conference. I know it's a constant interruption. Why not let his calls go to his voice mail and check it every hour so you can stay focused on your work?"

- "Myrna from Marketing seems to think our department is her social obligation each time she passes through. It is not rude to smile at her and go right back to work."

- "Just because the request came in by e-mail doesn't mean that the response is required within minutes. Your priorities are important. Unless the message is urgent, plan the best time for *you* to respond."

- "I noticed that toward the end of the day, you are playing major catch up. I used to struggle with managing priorities, but then took this great course. Would you like some time management suggestions from the pros?"

- "Bouncing between priorities can slow you down. Have you considered giving yourself a telephone-free time slot?"

- "Joseph can keep you on the phone until next week. I've learned to never ask him an open-ended question. Also, I begin my call by saying, 'I only have a few minutes, but I wanted to return your call quickly.'"

➡

- "Telephone tag is very time-consuming. The more specific your message, the better chance you have of getting a call back when you are available or of getting a message that ends the game."
- "I know you have project A as a priority, but Ali has encountered some setbacks with project B and needs extra help. Where are you with project A? Can you afford to take a few hours out to help Ali? We need to meet that deadline, too."
- "I know you handle customer complaints with great diplomacy. Eva has a similar style. You could free up some valuable time by training her to share that role."
- "This proposal just came in and is due in a few days. What can we clear from your schedule so you can run with this?"
- "I need this data by 5:00 p.m. Can you get this to me and still meet your other deadlines? If not, we need to find additional help or make some calls. We cannot afford to let any of these items fall through the cracks."
- "Establishing a timeline early with other personnel involved will save time later."

Organization

The Motivational Mindset

- Despite the occasional employee who can reach into a seemingly disorganized landslide of papers and pull out the appropriate item, most people function better when organized.
- A well-organized business, filing system (hard copy and computer), and workspace save time, money, and anguish.
- The office must be organized in a way that everyone can understand. No one person should be the only one who can find anything.
- Even the people who can keep everything in their heads without ever writing anything down get sick, win the lottery, move on. Good organization is something that can be picked up on by someone else when necessary.
- Improving organizational skills can improve time management and reduce stress. Obviously, scrambling to find things wastes time and, depending on the urgency of the item, can raise the stress level of everyone in the vicinity.
- Good organizational skills can also reduce the risk of missed deadlines or last-minute rushes.
- People with true organizational skills get things done. Others are so busy organizing that they spend more time arranging planners than doing actual work. Learn to recognize the difference so that you can support people and get them on the right track.
- Some people are very good at their jobs but are hindered by a lack of organization. Don't stifle creative people by saddling them with rigorous organizational systems,

but encourage everyone to use a system that works for them.

- Be open to new technology that can organize, synch calendars, and back up computer files. If your employees are more comfortable with new methods that would be improvements on the old, let them train you.
- For critical data, back up your backup.

Motivational Phrases

- "I like the way you organized the _____ office, filing system, data, team assignments. Thank you."
- "I am always impressed by how you keep things running so smoothly around here."
- "I'm sure your new organizational system is more streamlined than our old one, but we all need to understand how it works. Let's hold a meeting so you can explain the new system."
- "Many people on our team find it difficult to find files on the computer. Everyone seems to be using their own systems, leaving files scattered and hard to find. Let's work together to come up with a system that we can all use."
- "The business has been growing so fast, I think that's why certain things have slipped through the cracks. What ideas do you have for recreating organizational systems?"
- "Would you like to attend a class on organization to learn ways you can bring our office up to speed in light of our recent expansion? Check the training catalogue to see what's available."
- "What organizational system works best for you? You will be more inclined to stay with one that suits your style."
- "Keeping up with all the paperwork can be overwhelming.

➡

Several people found this _____ (course, system, process) useful. What do you think?"

- "You seem to have your finger on the pulse of any given moment's priority. What system do you use for keeping priorities in order?"
- "I realize this project is not on the A list because it's not time sensitive, but it *is* important. Do you have ideas about how to schedule this into the workday/week over the next few months?"
- "Please put your important dates on the master calendar. We all depend on each other at one time or another, so it is always helpful to know who will be here when and when others might or might not be available to offer support."
- "You must have been frustrated to have missed that meeting because of a computer glitch. Let's find software that keeps our calendars updated and synchronized."
- "Please be sure to keep everyone in your department posted when your contact information changes. We want clients and customers to know you have the strong support system you deserve."
- "Whom can I entrust with the responsibility of backing up the main database? None of us can afford the time it would take to track down lost data."
- "Everyone has a different process for organizing leads for follow up. Let's share so we can learn from one another."

Presentation Skills

The Motivational Mindset

- Many employees must present new ideas to their peers or to management; plans, proposals, or findings to other parts of the company; or company initiatives to existing or prospective clients.
- Presentation skills do not come naturally to everyone.
- Comfort and knowledge play key roles in effective presentations.
- Ensure that employees know that they've been selected to present or serve on a panel because of their knowledge. Praise their backgrounds and understanding of specific topics and issues, emphasizing that's why you've asked them to be out front.
- Build confidence through offering courses and/or opportunities for small group presentations with supportive feedback.
- Provide necessary equipment and tips on the most effective ways to use it.
- Encourage employees to watch strong, effective speakers on TV, videos, or in person.
- Have an instructional video available and offer basic tips online or in hard copy.
- Assure others that they can learn to relax, speak up, speak slowly and clearly, make eye contact, and connect with their audiences.
- Provide positive feedback and supportive suggestions for improvement. Encourage practice.

➡

Motivational Phrases

- "I'd like you to present our marketing plan to the management team. Are you comfortable?"
- "You know this product's features and benefits better than anyone. We need an additional rep at our booth at the national conference. Would you like some presentation skills coaching before that comes up?"
- "Your presentation last week was strong. I have a few suggestions to make you an even more effective speaker."
- "By using focused, dynamic gestures, you can strengthen your delivery."
- "I usually choose several friendly faces throughout the audience and make eye contact with them."
- "Remember, everyone is attending this meeting to learn about your _____ (approach, development, initiative, findings, recent meeting with XYZ…), not to criticize your presentation."
- "You would be surprised at how a smile warms up an audience."
- "I was very impressed with your handling of the Q and A. Your answers were succinct and to the point. Clearly, you were the expert in the room."
- "When you review your talk, eliminate unnecessary words, phrases, jargon, and irrelevant details."
- "Your soft-spoken manner tends to make people feel comfortable in one-to-one discussions, but you'll have to practice projecting when you make presentations, even at our committee meetings."
- "I noticed that your voice tightens when you speak up at meetings. Try drinking hot tea or coffee instead of cold water."

➡

- "Your presentations have become quite polished. My one suggestion is that you work on inflection."
- "I saw a very motivational speech on television last night. I taped it for anyone who would like to use it for pointers on presentation style." (Do not use religious or political figures. No matter how motivational they may be, when emotions get involved the points you hope to make will be lost.)
- "That was a tough Q and A that you fielded. One way to control the 'question bully' is to use eye contact and body language. As soon as you complete your answer, turn and acknowledge someone in another part of the room."
- "Wow! You were dynamic, well versed, and succinct. We could not have asked for a better representative."

Chapter 7

Motivational Challenges

"Others will underestimate us, for although we judge ourselves by what we feel capable of doing, others judge us only by what we have already done."

—Henry Wadsworth Longfellow

Motivational challenges can seem overwhelming at times. It's easy to say "I would be a great motivator, but how can anyone motivate under these circumstances? I'm supervising people who seem not to care, who are negative, are constantly complaining about the rules, or just don't get along." This is not the time to give up; you need to double your efforts to both motivate yourself and overcome these challenges to motivate others. Sometimes an employer must recognize a poor fit or realize that the employee cannot develop the requisite skills. The motivational employer can turn most employees around by tapping into the smallest window of opportunity to help them make positive changes. Norman Vincent Peale, author of *The Power of Positive Thinking*, wrote: "People become really quite remarkable when they start thinking that they can do things. When they believe in themselves, they have the first secret of success."

The diversity challenge is also ever-increasing. People who came up the ranks with a traditional hierarchy are working later in life and mixing at all levels with a new breed of young people who come in with strong skills and high expectations. The virtual commuter has been quickly finding where to fit into it all; and the current level of cultural diversity would have seemed extraordinary not long ago. Each category brings its own set of challenges.

A Culturally Diverse Workforce

The Motivational Mindset

- Ensure that everyone is treated equally. Do not tolerate discrimination based on *any* difference. Be aware of your own biases and limiting perceptions so that you can keep yourself in check, as well as others.

- The culturally diverse workforce has become the norm rather than the exception in many areas of the country. Just as a culturally homogeneous group benefits from diversities such as age or educational backgrounds, the culturally diverse workforce brings new benefits.

- Often, the diverse workforce reflects the customer base within that geographical area. Diversity within the workforce increases the organization's understanding of the customer.

- Whether a culturally diverse workforce is seen or experienced as an advantage is a matter of perspective. It does often present unique challenges and those who see any change as a downside will be quick to see diversity as a negative. Your job as motivator is to focus on the positive aspects and navigate the challenges.

- Take advantage of everyone's unique strengths. Respect differences and build on common values.

- Model and demand language and accent sensitivity. As possible, offer English classes for those who don't speak English and foreign language classes for those who supervise or manage employees with limited English abilities.

- English speakers can be discouraged and feel left out when bilingual employees are speaking other languages ➡

around them. Make clear that same-language communication among employees, when possible, is the ideal. Communication is challenging enough when we're all speaking the same language.

- Don't tell (or allow) jokes about race, religion, or nationality —including the joke-teller's own. Even when we can laugh at ourselves, telling those jokes gives mixed signals to others.
- The evolution of our workforce requires sensitivity to multiple holidays.
- Understand and explain, when necessary, that levels of eye contact and personal space are different in various cultures and that body language we would take as clear cues from Americans may not mean the same at all when expressed by someone from another culture.

Motivational Phrases

- "We're lucky to have such diversity among us. The more perspectives we have, the greater our advantage."
- "We will not tolerate racial or religious slurs. I've spoken with X. If anyone ever makes you uncomfortable again, please tell me so I can resolve the situation."
- "Many of our clients are not used to your accent. If you try speaking just a little bit more slowly you might notice a big difference in how well people understand. I know it's frustrating when you have to repeat yourself."
- "I understand that you feel like an outsider when you walk onto the dock and everyone is speaking Spanish, but you're only passing through and they all speak Spanish more comfortably than English. I'll talk to them about making you feel comfortable, but we need to think of their comfort, too."

- "We're offering English classes for employees and Spanish for supervisors."
- "Our workforce has changed dramatically. We will provide cultural diversity seminars to help each of us understand the nuances of one another's cultures."
- "When you order sandwiches for meetings, please select some vegetarian options, including nondairy, to ensure that there's something for everyone."
- "Tapas, I could use your help. I have a new client from India and I just came from a meeting that felt strained. I'm having trouble reading him. If I fill you in, can you tell me whether his reactions reflect cultural norms or whether I should be concerned?"
- "Nguyen is not showing disrespect by avoiding eye contact. Actually, in his culture, lack of eye contact is a sign of respect."
- "Personal space and comfort zones vary among different cultures. Let's work to raise our awareness out of respect for each other and our clients."
- "Our Hispanic customer base has increased significantly. In addition to our bilingual support staff, I strongly recommend our in-house Spanish for Business course for all managers and supervisors."
- "I realize that we can't all become proficient in the many languages of our housekeeping staff, but we can learn a few phrases in their languages to show that while they're struggling to learn English, we're trying, too."
- "We are adding glossaries to our upward mobility manuals to assist those attendees whose first language is not English."
- "You did the right thing by telling me about the offensive

➡

statements you overheard. I will talk with everyone who was there immediately and if it happens again, please do not hesitate to tell me. We have a zero tolerance policy for that kind of language and I'm sorry you were subjected to it."

- "Different cultures use different greetings. Mirror the greeting you receive."

Generations at Work

Four generations now share the workplace. They are often referred to as: The Silent Generation, Baby Boomers, Generation X, and Generation Next. In brief, the Silent Generation remembers when the executives were men (in dark suits and white shirts) and secretaries (in dresses and high heels) used old-fashioned typewriters, carbon paper, and microfiche. Baby Boomers raised the status of women in the workplace and changed traditional notions of family roles at home. Gen Xers grew up alongside the technology boom. They brought a wave of dress-down, flextime, work-at-home, and play-at-work attitudes to the office. Gen Nexters come to the table with technology as a second skin. The first rung on the corporate ladder is not always their first step. Their workplace is so different from the one where the Silent Generation got its start, that a Nexter might guess that *microfiche* is a small French fish. However, specific age groups and profiles of each group are less important than understanding some common issues that arise when generations come together at work.

The Motivational Mindset

- For a long time workplace advancement was guided by a simple, reliable formula: age = experience = opportunities for advancement. Being supervised by much younger people may be a difficult adjustment for many.
- If you look or are considered "too young" for your position, don't make threats or unreasonable power plays to show your strength. Most new managers need to earn respect. Being solid, rational, and doing what needs to be done will earn you that respect.

➥

- Young workers are starting out at salaries many senior employees would never have dreamed of at their ages. Sometimes a simple matter of economics can feel personal or feed resentment.
- Be open to the "voice of experience." Sometimes, you can save time and effort by building on a past approach or document and by learning about past pitfalls.
- If an older report is directly refusing to "answer to you" or making jokes about your age, initiate a frank discussion. If reasoning fails, deal with the action as you would any other disruptive, counterproductive behavior that does not belong in a business environment.
- If you're having trouble getting buy-in for your ideas from the "old guard," consider your presentation style and whether you put down the old methods that served their purpose well. Consider also whether you've given a reasonable time frame for transitions.
- Younger generations may feel frustrated when others are not as technologically savvy. Praise technological prowess, but encourage patience.
- Before you say, "We tried that 10 years ago; it didn't work," or "I know what works; I've tried it all," consider how much has changed. Could an approach that didn't work then have simply been before its time?
- Don't make people "pay their dues" on principle. Times, entry-level skills, competitive offerings, and expectations have changed.
- If you believe that younger workers don't respect experience, pause to consider whether *you* respect new ideas. If you believe older workers don't respect new ideas, pause to consider whether *you* respect experience.

➡

Motivational Phrases

- "I've been doing this so long I sometimes get stuck in my ways. I know you have a lot of great ideas. Let's schedule a time to sit down and talk about them."

- "Before you completely dismiss old methods, consider whether it might be best to build on them. Looking at all angles will ultimately make your idea stronger."

- "When suggesting something new, don't put down the old. Be careful in your phrasing. People may take it personally and feel put down. When you present new ideas, you don't want to start by putting people on the defensive."

- "Barbara has been here a long time. You will never gain her respect without showing yours."

- "I'm impressed with your training. It took me a few years in the business to get to the level you're at now."

- "Many management trainees in this company have the same level of technical skill that you have. Your way of making people feel valued is your unique edge."

- "The board is open to new ideas as long as they are presented in a traditional format. Observe another meeting as you prepare your presentation."

- "Seniority weighs very heavily with upper management. Get some experienced staffers on your side before you go in."

- "I understand that you're upset about senior employees who refer to you as 'kid.' Have you asked them not to? I'm sure they mean well and will make the effort to stop if you tell them it makes you uncomfortable. If you tell them and they continue, let me know."

- "I know you're eager to get ahead. We do carefully consider those with seniority when filling management ➡

positions. We are a very loyal company and that's one way we can show appreciation for those who have stuck with us over the years, but you do have upward mobility opportunities. Let's meet to talk about your future."

- "Please share your knowledge from prior experiences and work with us to determine what is relevant to our present circumstances."

- "When you resent a request or behavior by a young new employee, consider whether your expectation or judgment is based on your own past experience. Ask yourself whether the belief you formed is still valid. Is your expectation reasonable at this time?"

- "Before you resent not being approached for advice or expertise, consider whether you've made yourself available. Let others know that you're eager to help and that their questions are not an imposition."

- "I know you're upset about Keri getting an expense account after only three months when you were here for six years before you got one. It's no longer a matter of status—it's practicality. She entertains clients, we have room in the budget, and these accounts cut down on bookkeeping."

- "I know you cringe when Jake calls you 'old timer.' Have you told him? I know that he respects you, and he may just think of it as a friendly nickname. I'm sure he'll stop if you tell him it makes you uncomfortable. If not, let me know."

The Underachiever

Underachiever can have two distinct meanings. One sends your overnight package, but doesn't follow up to see that it arrived. The other sends your package overnight, follows up to see that it arrived, and has at hand the name of the person he or she spoke to. That second person (who follows up), if resistant when offered a promotion, would be referred to by many as an underachiever. However, in that job, daily, that person is achieving high-quality performance. Let's call that person the *career underachiever* and let's call the underachiever who doesn't follow up on the overnight package and doesn't seem to care the *blasé underachiever*.

The Motivational Mindset
(for the blasé underachiever)

- Some people feel overwhelmed or have trouble looking at the big picture and seeing where to begin. Help by breaking down large projects into smaller, manageable tasks.

- Some underachievers may never have been appreciated or told that their work made any significant contribution. Or, they may have learned how to just "get by" years ago and may come alive if inspired by some spark of interest.

- You might be supervising someone who has felt "used by the system" in the past and is on the defensive regarding his or her personal time and space. Show that you are not going to take advantage, and you may see the individual's defenses come down and work performance improve.

- Explain how the employee fits in with the organization and the importance of the job he or she is doing.

- Give developmental feedback. Don't worry so much about crushing the spirit of the blasé underachiever that you ➡

refrain from giving solid, developmental feedback. Such feedback has the potential to turn around an apparent lack of motivation and follow through.

■ Clarify your expectations and give clear direction. Often, people don't realize the little steps that complete a job.

■ Be diligent about praising even small, positive changes and jobs well done.

■ Assess whether additional training in a particular skill set will improve confidence, abilities, and drive.

■ Encourage attendance at professional conferences.

■ Examine whether a person is over- or underqualified. Sometimes someone is just the wrong fit for the job.

Motivational Phrases
(for the blasé underachiever)

■ "You tend to procrastinate routine tasks. Why do you think that is?"

■ "What do you enjoy most about your work day?"

■ "You have so much talent, but something seems to be holding you back. I'd like to discuss this with you. Is there anything I can do?"

■ "You say you're getting bored with your job. What changes would motivate you?"

■ "What would make this job (or specific task) more interesting/challenging for you?"

■ "You seem overwhelmed by this project. Why not break it down? Where would you start?"

■ "I know that _____ is repetitive work, but without it, our department would be in big trouble."

■ "Small steps lead to great achievements."

■ "Your role in our organization is more valuable than

➡

you may realize. When you walk past any customer during your day, please smile and say, 'Hello.' Your interactions are important."

- "Never lose your long-range vision."
- "A clean environment is important to everyone. That makes your role particularly important."
- "It may seem like a small thing, but greeting _____ (guests, tenants, shoppers, clients…) makes a big difference."
- "I appreciate your staying on top of routine maintenance problems. You save us time and the company money."
- "I was impressed with the way you handled _____ (the crowd, the complaint, the confusion…) today. Good work!"

The Motivational Mindset
(for the career underachiever)

- Be certain that employees are *aware* of possible upward moves and their access to steps that lead there.
- Always ask when you see potential, and encourage if you see a glimmer of interest. However, don't make a mission out of making your dreams come true for someone else. Respect employees' choices and let them feel good about where they are.
- Some people have enough and don't want more. They don't need the bigger paycheck or want more hours *or* responsibility. They are where they are for a reason—it's where they want to be.
- The *career underachiever* is like the big fish in a little pond—highly successful in the present position and seemingly overqualified with wasted talents. If someone is

➡

happy in a position and doesn't want to change, what does *wasted* mean? A promotion could mean longer hours, less time at home, or less contact with people all day. You have to know what someone enjoys in order to motivate.

- Never hold someone back, but show your appreciation for those who choose to stay where they are. If someone is doing a highly competent job and wants to stay put, be happy for that employee and grateful to have such a competent person in that position.

- There are no small parts on any business stage. Whether someone is working behind the scenes or out in front of clients or customers, everyone has some impact on how the product functions, how it's packaged, how the customer sees the company, or the morale of other employees around them. Everyone has some impact. Make sure everyone knows the importance of his or her role.

- For the *career underachiever* who does not realize his or her potential, your role in noticing, acknowledging, and encouraging that potential is critical.

- Confidence and self-esteem may be issues for both the *blasé underachiever* and the *career underachiever*.

- Positive feedback is important for everyone, but may make all the difference for an underachiever.

- Be sensitive to the *career underachiever's* underlying motivation. Avoid variations of "What's a smart girl like you doing in a joint like this?"

Motivational Phrases
(for the career underachiever)

- "In what ways do you think your job could be more challenging?"

➡

- "What do you enjoy most about your current position?"
- "You have so much talent, but something seems to be holding you back. Would you like to discuss it?"
- "You have tremendous ability. I'd love to have you continue assisting me, but I'd like to help you go further in the organization."
- "You seem happy in your present job; however, I see potential for promotion to the next level. Does this interest you?"
- "Your work is outstanding! Would you be interested in taking steps toward moving up?"
- "A position for _____ is opening up and I think you would be ideal."
- "What training, resources, information, or skills would make you comfortable in moving to the next level?"
- "You know I value your contribution to our department, but your _____ skills could help you take off. Do you want to know about other opportunities in the organization?"
- "You have such a good grasp of the floater's role. Would you consider training others?"
- "Your understanding of this process is beyond that of most in your position. Would you be interested in working on a handbook?"
- "You've managed every department in the store successfully. There's an opening in our San Francisco branch for a store manager. Would you like to discuss what's involved?"
- "What are your career goals?"
- "Most of our managers started _____ (in sales, as cashiers, behind the counter…). Let's look at an upward mobility path that suits your skills and abilities."

The Powerhouse Overachiever

As with underachievers, you will find a few types of over-achievers. Of course, many super-achievers work like whirling dervishes, efficiently making things happen all in a day's work without paying a toll. However, some overachievers are motivational challenges. Some will do just about anything to achieve and can wreak havoc on workplace harmony. (We'll call these *reckless overachievers*.) Others will work beyond their own limits at the risk of sacrificing health and well-being, which, in the end, isn't good for anyone. (We'll call these *workaholic overachievers*.)

The Motivational Mindset
(for the reckless overachiever)

- While overachievers can be wonderfully productive, they may also be so focused on the prize they miss slowing down for critical details. Their good efforts should be recognized, even when they need to be reminded to check for accuracy.

- When accuracy is essential, a system of checks and balances should be in place that applies to everyone. Help the overachiever understand that this is the standard process because mistakes can and do happen to everyone, and we're all too close to our own work to see certain things.

- Overachievers may be more focused on the next job than the one they're in now.

- Overachievers may be critical of others who are working at a different pace.

- The overachiever may have maxed out at his/her skill level. If Sasha is an outstanding salesperson with no

➡

patience for those learning the ropes, don't promote her to sales supervisor. Give strong reinforcement that she is valued as the right person for her current position.

■ The overachiever who is told that it's okay to slow down may be relieved. Some people push beyond reasonable limits to meet wrongly assumed expectations.

■ Overachievers may want the next position so badly that they will plow ahead without pausing for training or asking questions. When delegating, be clear about the importance of checkpoints and questions during the learning process.

■ Do not allow employees to self-impose a supervisory role over others.

Motivational Phrases
(for the reckless overachiever)

■ "Great work! Did everyone on the team get a chance to review it?"

■ "Thank you for working so late last night. This is outstanding work! I know that your team members were geared up to work on this during business hours. Please show this to them to review and finalize the details together. Again, great work, but I encourage you not going it alone next time."

■ "I appreciate the work you did on project Q. At the same time, I still need project A completed by 3 p.m., Thursday. How is that coming? A is the priority now and if you can put in the same energy you put into Q we'll be in great shape. Thanks."

■ "I can't believe how quickly you finished the inventory! As you know, accuracy is critical. Did you check it over? Has anyone else helped you with a final check?"

➡

- "I expected that repair to continue into next week. Well done! Take a long lunch. You deserve it."
- "I know how well you can multitask. Often, it's necessary. When serving a customer, though, the best course is to focus on the customer. Almost anything else can wait."
- "I notice that you posted for department manager. I hope you get the job. I'd be happy to chat with you about what you might expect in that role."
- "I'm sure you know that there's a sales manager position opening. Your sales skills are outstanding and produce great income for you and the company. I hope you decide to stay in your active role on the sales team. I don't see you behind a desk pushing papers."
- "One of Martin's clients told him you said he was unavailable yesterday, but he never knew the call came in. Yes, we're in a competitive industry, but trust among colleagues is important. Your last company may have done things differently, but I think you will enjoy the benefits of the cooperative environment we've created."
- "You were right about the return policy and your jumping in was important. However, I encourage you to be more tactful when correcting a coworker, especially in front of a customer."
- "We have a system in this restaurant. If someone cannot get to a table immediately, we pitch in, but we don't take over tables in someone else's section. That creates a competitive environment that doesn't benefit staff or customers."
- "I know that the balance has been weighted more heavily on your shoulders lately. Thank you for stepping up."
- "You completed the inventory ahead of schedule; however, you overlooked some categories. Speed without

➡

accuracy is not fast. With your abilities, you can slow down and still stay ahead of schedule."

- "Tom, you've been spending a lot of time talking with people in the Finance Department. When there's an opening, that's a good move for you and I'll support it. Right now, Marketing needs all your energy."

- "Suzanne, I understand your drive to complete each project and move to the next. That's a great work ethic; however, we have an editing protocol that everyone— even top-notch writers like you—must follow. Please help me out."

The Motivational Mindset
(for the workaholic overachiever)

- These overachievers may be so dedicated to being "all they can be" for the organization that they are neglecting personal relationships and/or themselves.

- The *workaholic overachiever* will eventually burn out.

- Work-life balance is as important to forward-looking companies as it is to employees.

- Don't punish competence by placing a much heavier workload on the one who is getting things done.

- While some overachievers can be careless, missing details in their rush to get more done, some present the opposite challenge of pushing themselves to be perfect. Your role includes reminding them of the time factor and that cooked is better than overcooked."

- If someone is suddenly burying him/herself in work and insists this is the best course of action "for now," don't take advantage by setting the bar to that new level of output.

- Beware of taking the overachiever for granted. When

➡

someone is *consistently* doing good work quickly, don't underestimate the value of *consistent* praise and recognition.

■ Some workaholics run on stress; others are running *from* personal stress. Don't play shrink, but be aware of motivation.

■ *Workaholic overachievers* may glow when burning the midnight oil, but if they are not careful, they could burn out their staff.

■ The *workaholic overachiever*, if unaware of his/her style and its drawbacks, can be a detriment in a management position.

Motivational Phrases
(for the workaholic overachiever)

■ "I notice you've worked every night this week. That must be difficult with the new baby at home."

■ "You do fantastic work all day long. I hope you don't take the problems of the day home with you."

■ "I don't want to pry, but when do you get time for you and your family? I'm ecstatic about your dedication, but I hope you realize that the organization also respects your need for work-life balance."

■ "I know how dedicated you are to the monthly accounting, but your long hours here during your post-op period are more than anyone should handle. Let's get a temp to help you."

■ "I know you've been late in the mornings because you have been working late. I wish we could offer comp time, but we can't right now and we need your high energy in the mornings."

➡

- "I notice that you've been taking shorter and shorter lunches. I hope you know how much I appreciate the quality of your work. Your eating a leisurely lunch will not put the company in jeopardy. I care about your health as well as your work."
- "You look exhausted. How late were you here last night? Don't make me set a curfew!"
- "We're growing too fast, but the solution is not for you to become superhuman. I do appreciate your trying!"
- "The promotion means longer hours and travel. I know you can handle it, but I also know that you have a new family. This position fits your work goals, but I want you to feel certain that it also fits your life and family goals. I will support any decision you make."
- "Your redesign of the Orientation Program and related manual and visual aids is phenomenal. I know that you and your staff put in many late nights. Our budget allows for a celebration lunch. I also urge you to let them work at only 110 percent for the next few weeks."
- "Your energy is inspiring! Keep a little in reserve and take care of yourself. We need you strong for the long haul."
- "Thank you so much for that extra effort. It really paid off."
- "What made you stay late last night to double-check the number of giveaways for the trade show? Boy, did you save us!"
- "You put in a great day's work. Go home and relax!"

The Part-Time Employee

The Motivational Mindset

- The part-time employee needs to feel as much a part of the team as the full-time staff. A part-time commitment is still a commitment.
- Ensure that part timers know that their roles are critical to customer satisfaction and company success.
- Include part-time employees as much as possible in office meetings and celebrations.
- Mentors help part timers learn their jobs and help them see their work in the context of the larger picture.
- Some organizations are entirely staffed by part timers because of customer needs or business demands.
- Part timers may be overqualified but need the scheduling convenience of part-time work. Know who's working in your midst and access talent.
- Consider small incentives. Offer a gift card or cash reward for perfect on-time attendance, outstanding customer service, or any other one-time or ongoing behavior you would like to reinforce.
- Ensure that part-time employees have all the information they need to represent your company or department effectively. Don't just give them "need to know" information.
- Often part timers report to more than one supervisor. Ensure a consistent message regarding work, policies, and customer care. Also ensure that all supervisors understand the need to coordinate priorities when sharing the support of a part timer.
- Share with your part timers the mechanics behind juggling schedules. Part-time work is not a casual commitment.

➡

Motivational Phrases

- "Please give as much notice as possible if you have to change your schedule. You're part of a team, so your schedule affects others."
- "Thanks for always leaving such clear notes for those who work the next shift."
- "Although you are only here three days each week, your effect on the _____ (patients, residents, customers, guests…) is noticeable."
- "Thank you for your contributions to the project."
- "Please feel free to ask questions. I want you to understand the process."
- "I called you in to give you this gift card as a bonus. You're always here on schedule, on time, always ready to do what's needed. Keep up the good work!"
- "Each month you will be eligible for a 'perfect on-time attendance' bonus. Changing your schedule with 24-hour notice will not affect eligibility."
- "You're doing an excellent job. If you become interested in a full-time position here, I would be happy to help you find one."
- "I'm very impressed by what you are able to accomplish within a part-time schedule."
- "Most of the staff is part time. Part timers are our backbone."
- "Because we have a number of part-time sales associates, we have established a system for sharing customer inquiries and complaints. Following it carefully simplifies everyone's job."
- "All of our blackjack dealers pool their tips. I know not every casino does this, but that's our policy. It has resulted in ➡️

improved customer service and larger tips for everyone."
- "Thank you for agreeing to work Saturdays."
- "I know that Tuesday/Thursday has been your schedule for years. Would you consider helping out Sobie by trying Wednesday/Thursday for a few months?"
- "Even though you are not here full time, your work product has full-time value."

The Virtual Commuter

The Motivational Mindset

- These days, entire offices may be virtual.
- Though working offsite has become an acceptable standard for many, transitioning from the traditional office may be difficult.
- Virtual commuting can be combined with physical office time.
- Many managers are satisfied as long as the work gets done. Hours logged may be less important than results.
- Unique communication issues arise between virtual commuters and those working in-house. You will need to be sensitive to these.
- Virtual commuters should be treated with the same respect and support as people who are physically there.
- If the number of hours logged by an offsite employee is important, create a uniform, consistent system for recording.
- Some people in the office may treat the offsite employee as a second-class citizen; it is important that everyone understand the virtual commuter is an important part of the team.
- Just as those in the office periodically chat, an occasional friendly e-mail, instant message, or telephone chat with the virtual commuter is good for mental health and team spirit.
- If you, as a supervisor, are the virtual commuter, make yourself as accessible as possible.

➡

Motivational Phrases

- "You are as much a part of this team as anyone who is physically in the office, and you are entitled to support."
- "Please sync your schedule with the office's online calendar."
- "Please give support staff as much lead time as possible to integrate your priorities into their schedules. In order for them to keep you in the scheduling loop, you need to keep them in yours."
- "Sometimes, some of you seem to forget that Raul is part of the team. Please remember that it's not 'Raul's project'; it is *our* project and is just as important as others on the table."
- "Our Thursday morning staff meetings are a great energy exchange. We'll make arrangements to conference you in."
- "Our monthly staff meetings are the best way for you to stay connected and for everyone to get to know you. Please make them a top priority."
- "Please check with Sally before you choose a format or font. When integrating your work is time-consuming, everyone gets frustrated."
- "You can't see our smiles, but that design is awesome."
- "That number crunching was dynamite. Thank you for getting it to us so quickly."
- "You've been having some problems with your server. Please call our service company today. A major project is coming your way in a few days."
- "You seem to have instinctively fit right into the virtual commuter role. Would you consider training others?"
- "Getting in tune with the time difference is a challenge. Our project planning chart accounts for that to ensure ➡"

that no one is waiting for material while someone is sleeping."

- "Don't feel guilty about working in the sunshine. We have other advantages, like cafeteria food."
- "We will miss you when you move. Please consider the virtual commuting option."
- "You are our first virtual commuter, so please don't be discouraged by any little snags in the system. I'm sure we can work them out as we all adjust."

The Naysayer

The Motivational Mindset

- The naysayer can affect the energy and motivation of a team.
- Don't fall into the trap of treating the naysayer as the boy who cried wolf. Sometimes there really is a wolf.
- Positive attitudes spread; so do negative ones.
- Sometimes, the naysayer just needs to be validated and will be willing to come onboard after feeling heard and appreciated.
- Often, naysayers are unaware of the frequency and/or impact of their negative comments.
- Model for others ways to deflect the naysayer's comments.
- Offer suggestions and model ways for the naysayer to turn negative approaches or phrases into positive ones.
- Talk with the naysayer about his/her negativity (using specifics) and its effect on others.
- Understand that you may not be able to encourage someone to change an ingrained habit or personality trait. However, the positive environment you create will help bring balance and may begin to turn the naysayer around.

Motivational Phrases

- "I appreciate your voicing reasonable concerns, but once we decide to move forward, we need positive support."
- "I understand the problems you've pointed out and your concerns are valid. What solutions can you offer and what data do you have to support them?"
- "We get back what we put out. Let's put out some positive energy."

➡️

- "Often, your questions ensure that we explore all options. This time, however, we have time constraints and strong reasons to go forward. Can you suspend your doubts in order for us all to put high energy into making this work?"
- "I understand your reservations. Let's review the pros and cons."
- "Your team's work product is outstanding. I agree with you about the need for some modification, but when you present this idea at the management meeting, please focus on all the positive elements and mention the minor changes after generating enthusiasm."
- "You know how shy Maria is. She rarely offers suggestions at meetings. Your criticizing her idea as she spoke not only clammed her up but prevented our learning more about her proposal. I'm sure you didn't intend to stop her cold. How might you have handled that differently?"
- "I know Harry will find a chink in the armor, but please stand your ground. This is a great proposal."
- "I know you have some doubts, but what do you think is valuable about our new security system?"
- "The management team's plan seems to cover all bases. Do you agree?"
- "Where do you think we fell short? What could we have done differently?"
- "Others would be more responsive to your valuable suggestions if you precede them with a positive statement about what is right."
- "Rather than jump in with a 'better idea,' why not ask your reports how they might make this work more effectively?"

➡

- "Implementing a new, company-wide accounting system is a daunting task. Despite the learning curve it will save us time and money. I'm counting on you to focus on the positive when you present the change-over to your staff."

Complaints About the Rules

The Motivational Mindset

- Rules, policies, procedures, and informal guidelines should be governed by logic and support your organization's values, mission, and goals.
- If "Because I said so" was frustrating as a kid, it's even more frustrating as an adult. Give cogent reasons, not flip responses.
- If someone requests that rules be bent for a good reason, be flexible. Reconsider the rule or consider carefully why this could be an exception.
- You may have a policy allowing a certain number of days off after the death of a family member, but if a dedicated worker needs more time, the bottom line is that we're all human behind those policies and sometimes we need a little understanding.
- If a request is made for a particularly good reason, but the exception cannot be made for everyone, explain your decision.
- Don't apply rules to some and not others. Favoritism de-motivates.
- Of course, if breaking a rule for one would cause a problem, stand your ground. But don't underestimate employees who might be more understanding than you think of a clearly explained exception.
- The more involved employees are in creating policies and procedures, the more interested they are in supporting them. Include those directly affected in determining and enforcing informal guidelines (e.g., keeping the coffee room neat, starting meetings on time, covering others' phones). ➡

- Some rules are dated or, without context, may seem random. People will be more likely to respect rules that make sense to them.
- Work to get ineffective and/or outdated rules changed. Explain what you're trying to accomplish.
- Safety policies are inviolate. These are "no exceptions" rules.

Motivational Phrases

- "The reason behind this rule is _____."
- "I'm sorry I cannot make an exception here. I have considered it carefully. I wish I could."
- "Please give me all the reasons you think we can or should make an exception in your case so that I can give your request thorough consideration."
- "A lot of people seem to have a problem with this rule. It was designed for a specific purpose. (Be clear about the purpose.) If anyone has ideas about how to modify this rule while maintaining its ability to achieve that purpose, I would be happy to consider them."
- "This rule ensures everyone's safety during an emergency evacuation. We cannot bend it—ever."
- "I know safety goggles sometimes seem unnecessary; however, we count on your vision in many ways and don't want to jeopardize it."
- "Privacy rules may be inconvenient at times, but we all appreciate them when our own privacy is at stake."
- "Since 9/11 we lock the courtyard door. The need for a convenient place to smoke does not supercede everyone's safety."
- "Yes, we can bend that rule in this case."

- "You have gone above and beyond so many times. I would be happy to make this request for you."
- "With technology changing daily, we must keep pace with privacy rules."
- "The occasional call to check on a lunch date or a child at home is fine. Lengthy personal phone calls are not. I'm sure you understand why."
- "I know it seems like a lot of red tape, but we have legal issues to consider."
- "I agree that the single earring per ear rule is dated. The dress code was established in 1991. No one has updated it. Human Resources is revising the guidelines."
- "That's a great outfit for a private party or dinner out. However, bare midriffs are not appropriate in this office."

Employee Conflicts

The Motivational Mindset

- Conflict thrives in an atmosphere of self-interest, unrealistic expectations, unfounded assumptions, poor communication, and limited access to information.
- Unchecked conflict leads to stress, polarization, and mistrust, creating an unproductive work environment.
- When conflict arises among employees, always get all sides of the story so that you can mediate logically and fairly. Describe or recap the situation succinctly, and ask all parties involved what result they would like to see.
- Leave your personal biases of what you think must have happened outside the door.
- Specify what you will do or what you would like to have happen.
- Don't be one to spread rumors—or listen to them. Make clear that the rumor mill is not a viable communication vehicle.
- Model and encourage respectful behavior, rational dialogue, and discussion of different points of view.
- Don't pit one employee against another or encourage rivalries. You have more positive vehicles to promote a drive for excellence.
- Address problems without blame.
- *Never* yell or curse.

Motivational Phrases

- "Excuse me; may I see you in my office, please?" (instead of public reprimands)
- "I have received complaints that you _____

➡

(shouted at Dan in front of customers, wouldn't share quarterly figures with Andrea…). I'd like to hear your side."

- "Jake, what I hear you saying is that you think Maya intentionally stole your client. Is that correct? Maya, you said you didn't know that this was Jake's client. Is that correct? Let's get to the bottom of this. What happened when the call came in? What can you do now to move forward with this client and to prevent this misunderstanding from occurring again?"

- "I understand you're upset, but I cannot focus on what you're saying when you are shouting."

- "You were both rushing. Isn't it possible that you misunderstood each other?"

- "Let's start with the assumption that no one lied. Misinformation and misperceptions do not mean someone intended to deceive. If we're going to get to the bottom of this, let's start by giving everyone the benefit of the doubt and see where that leads."

- "Clearly, you each have a different perception of what happened. Please tell me yours."

- "The situation, as I understand it, is this: _____. What resolution does each of you propose?"

- "I can see the anxiety this has caused. Let's slow down and look at the facts. We all want this to succeed."

- "Colin, what did you hear Jack say? Jack, what do you remember saying?"

- "It doesn't matter whose fault the mistake was. Let's pull together to fix the problem and determine how to prevent a similar one."

- "It was my mistake. I'm sorry for the extra work it caused."

- "We are all under a great deal of pressure; however,

➡

shouting at one another and slamming papers down on desks doesn't help. No one here is the problem. Let's focus on the work and be respectful of each other in the process."

- "I realize that Sven did not include you in the initial planning meeting. That would upset me also. Sven, you can understand that, right? However, now we must move on. What remaining issues must you address? You two can certainly work that out."

- "I can see both sides. How would each of you like to resolve this?"

Chapter 8

Raising Morale in Tough Times

"If you would lift me up you must be on higher ground."
—Ralph Waldo Emerson

The difference between working for one bank, department store, or manufacturer and another used to be minimal. Most people stayed with a company throughout their entire work life, many earning gold watches for 25 years of service. Stability was a virtue: the *company man* stayed put and the company remained *the company*. Today, as companies merge, acquire, and disappear, any sense of a stable work environment is challenged. When the company cannot guarantee that it—or you—will be there, you tend to look for that next place to land. The wise employer maintains a pulse check for signs of career dissatisfaction and keeps lines of communication open. Lack of information during challenging times leaves people frustrated and, often, assuming the worst of all possible scenarios.

Catching people before they fall, fail, or leave maintains a positive environment during the most trying times. Monica Smiley, publisher of *Enterprising Women*, sees a "common thread among the country's top women business owners: the ability to persevere in the face of daily adversity." Successful leaders in all business cultures bring that entrepreneurial spirit and the mindset to *tough it out* to any challenge. Susan Brenner, senior vice president of Bright Horizons Family solutions, advises: "It's easy to get mired in the day-to-day problems of the job and lose sight of the work's purpose. Look beyond the details, and remember the reason you do what you do, the goodness of your work. Then take on the daily issues, knowing that they are necessary steps to reaching your goals."

Transitions

The Motivational Mindset

- Mergers and acquisitions are major transitions. In the event of a merger or acquisition, you *can* set the tone as to how the news is received. Set a positive one.
- If your company is acquired by one that it has publicly criticized, don't pretend there was never any bad blood. You're not fooling anyone. Talk about where you are *now*, what has changed, and what makes you believe this union will bring specific improvements.
- Avoid surprises. Share information. Missing and misinformation fuel the rumor mill.
- Don't just toss out facts for general consumption. Think about those receiving the information. What is important for employees to know? What information is threatening to employees? Hold meetings; answer what questions you can.
- Stay positive, but don't sugarcoat reality.
- Plan your message; don't improvise.
- Deliver the news and move on—but be prepared to revisit the topic as delayed reactions occur and additional questions arise.
- When someone leaves the company for positive reasons, celebrate in a way that lets people say goodbye. Most employees form strong bonds at work. A coworker or colleague's leaving constitutes a major change.
- Fresh initiatives, a new name, and a new logo may breathe fresh air into the atmosphere, but if management does not follow through, the air quickly gets stale and people feel let down. Future initiatives will seem meaningless ➡

and are unlikely to find buy-in among people who have come to see them as the *flavor of the month*.

- If you start something new, be fully committed to it. If it's not working, fix it. Drop it if you have to, but don't let it fade away. Acknowledge what came out of it and explain why you're dropping it. Then move on.

Motivational Phrases

As always, say only what is true. This can be a tricky situation if corporate policy restricts what you can say. Use the following phrases if they apply.

- "We need your help through this tough time. If you can hang in with us, when we get back on track and our numbers are better, we will all benefit."
- "I know change is difficult. If you have any questions during the transition, please feel free to ask." (or refer questions to the appropriate person)
- "I know how much you value everyone in your department. You've built a great team. Whomever you decide to let go will be a loss for us all."
- "We are doing everything we can to reduce your stress during the acquisition process. Additional suggestions are welcome."
- "We will all miss Karthik. He was our top performer and a great guy. As we restructure, the field is wide open for new top performers. I hope you will all join me in looking to the future."
- "Please disregard the conflicting rumors about why Ari left the company. Of course, the rumor mill is not the most reliable place to get information. I'm sure Ari shared the reasons at his own discretion."

➡

- "We have gone through a lot of changes. Change can cause stress, but it also can bring opportunities."
- "I would like your input on our new direction."
- "The layoffs will not affect your job."
- "I've always been honest with you and will continue to be. Clearly, we will have some staff reassignments. That's not always a bad thing. I'll share what I learn as soon as I can."
- "I have talked with senior management about the crowded working conditions during the renovation. Unfortunately, so much is top priority right now that, although we have their ear and understanding, nothing will happen as quickly as we'd like."
- "Our informal management style is quite different from that of our new parent company. Please try to understand that they are bringing a style that has worked for them. In time, we might see the changes as beneficial overall."
- "You can all expect to be interviewed by the new management team. Be honest in your answers. If you believe that a process or policy has been a problem, say so. Also, champion what you think we're doing right or they won't know and it could change."
- "The acquisition process is lengthy. You can expect focus groups and individual interviews as the new management team learns about our processes and you, the people who made this company so successful."
- "Our company is in a position to make most personnel decisions. We will, however, be building a hybrid team that represents both companies. I appreciate all of you and your contributions and will do everything I can to retain you."

The Motivational Mindset

- Expect mature, rational responses. What you expect is often what you get.
- Avoid the urge to be a cliché dispenser. "Buck up" and "It's always darkest before the dawn" won't help anyone.
- Be as honest as you can be about why firing or layoff decisions were made.
- If you are cutting the dental plan, present possible resources for reasonably priced alternatives.
- In supporting employees, never bash upper management. Usually they are doing the best they can with the cards they were dealt. Undermining confidence in their leadership stresses the process.
- In supporting management, never put down employees or make them feel devalued. Explain how their participation in the process is essential to success.
- If you are cutting benefits or perks, always be clear that the decision is driven by economics, not performance.
- Explain the rationale behind across-the-board cuts or salary freezes. Be sensitive to the effects a hiring freeze will have on those already carrying a heavy load.
- Enlist staff support when deciding upon equipment/ material costs. They are usually the experts.
- If you are taking raises while employees are getting fired for economic reasons and facing cuts in pay or benefits, there are no words you can say. People will feel slighted, undervalued, and resentful. Many will be looking to move on.

➡

Motivational Phrases

As always, say only what is true. This can be a tricky situation if you are restricted by corporate policy in what you can say. Use the following phrases if they apply.

- "We can no longer afford _____, but we can offer you _____. I know that you deserve more, but this is the best we can do right now."
- "We have to temporarily cut back on overtime opportunities because of our current economic situation. I have every confidence we will be able to restore it within the year."
- "I wish we could pay you what you're worth."
- "The company values your contributions."
- "We can't provide raises this year, but we can look at flextime options to ease the situation."
- "I know we're understaffed right now, but there is nothing we can do about that at this time. We just have to pull together and do our best. I appreciate your efforts during this trying time."
- "I wish I could tell you the layoffs would not affect our department. I am as much in the dark as you are. As soon as I hear anything, you will."
- "All we can do is stay positive and put out our best work. To the best of my knowledge, our department is not in danger of layoffs."
- "We have to cut dental benefits, but I have a list of resources for low-cost alternatives. Benefits will be effective through June."
- "In order to continue providing health insurance, we've had to raise the co-pay. I'm sorry, but rates have skyrocketed and we want to be able to continue coverage for everyone."

➡

- "Okay, so the memo titled, 'Blue skies are gonna clear up' was corny, but at least management is trying."
- "I was trying to grow my business too fast during tough economic times, but I would hate to lose you. Would you consider buying in with sweat equity as a partner?"
- "We cannot offer holiday bonuses this year. I hope the days off with pay during the holiday season soften the blow for everyone."
- "Summers are becoming very slow. Would anyone like an additional week off at half pay?"
- "You know I can't offer you an increase, but I will work with you to ensure some additional time off."

The Motivational Mindset

- Hold meetings to address concerns.
- Disclose only what is allowable, but answer questions honestly.
- If the company's actions were immoral or illegal, don't defend them. Talk about changes and what it will take to make corrections and move forward.
- If someone in the company or an executive of the company was wrongly accused, inspire support from the ranks.
- Even if the company or executive were in the wrong, inspire support for the work to be done to turn the situation around and retain (or regain) respect in the community.
- You may lose some people along the way. It's to be expected.
- Do not allow whistleblowers to be abused. Even if you disagree with their actions, even if they could have used other channels, and even if their suspicions were wrong, these are usually not people who want to hurt anyone. In fact, their motivation is likely to protect as many people as possible, and they risk their own comfort to do so.
- Be a model of ethical behavior, no matter what's happening around you.
- Clearly follow your company's legal and public relations guidelines when addressing employees.
- Inform employees of legal and public relations guidelines to ensure their compliance.

Motivational Phrases

- "Do you have any questions?"

- "We need your support during this difficult time."
- "We have made mistakes." (*If* you're allowed to say that, say it.)
- "We've been hearing a lot about what's *wrong* with the company and we have people working on that. Let's work on faith that they're doing their jobs and continue to do ours. Let's be what's *right* with this company."
- "Let's generate some *positive* press."
- "Let's explore ideas for positive things we can do to rebuild trust _____ (in our company, within the community, among clients and stockholders…)."
- "We are at a crossroads, about to enter unknown territory. We need your intuition and creativity more than ever before."
- "Let's not give power to the rumor mill. Please hold off on making judgments until we have all the facts."
- "Setbacks are an opportunity for reevaluating strategy and trying new ideas."
- "The news may be skewed for sensationalism. Let's focus on what we know is real."
- "Let's ignore the headlines and keep a clear perspective."
- "We would like to take responsibility for where we've gone wrong and go forward in a positive direction. We need your help in creating a positive, forward-thinking environment."
- "Setbacks are opportunities to develop new strategies and create fresh starts."
- "You will be besieged by family and friends for 'the dirt.' Please use discretion in discussing information and focus on the company-wide effort to turn this problem around."
- "We don't have time for 'management bashing.' We, in the trenches, are fighting to redeem the company's image."

The Motivational Mindset

- If people aren't meeting your expectations or they seem frustrated or overworked, ask yourself whether your expectations are reasonable. If you were in their positions, would you be making the sacrifices you're asking them to make?
- Are the lead times you give before deadlines realistic?
- Look at the company, your offerings, the skill levels you have hired, and current workplace trends.
- If your expectations are unreasonable, no amount of motivation will sustain a workforce's exhilaration in the task of climbing uphill.
- People need goals they can meet and small successes they can achieve daily or weekly.
- If your employees are continually failing, look at ways to motivate, but also look at their realistic chances for success within the parameters given to them.
- Are people putting a negative buzz in the air every day? Why?
- Do the surroundings feel conducive to success? Or would someone describe them as bleak or run down? It doesn't take much to get a coat of paint on the walls, hang something cheerful, or get a few plants.
- Did you just renovate and now everyone seems to be hitting a slump, with some suddenly out sick more than usual? Sick building syndrome is real and certain chemicals can cause *brain fog* or a myriad of other physical symptoms. If you've just painted or put in new carpeting or walls, air out the area well and consider an air filter, especially if you don't have windows.

➡

- Maintain your enthusiasm and support others in rediscovering theirs.

Motivational Phrases

- "What problems interfere with your meeting deadlines?"
- "What do you believe held you back from completing this project on time?"
- "What skills do you believe you need to develop through additional training in order to meet our goals?"
- "Let's brainstorm ideas to get some energy back into this operation."
- "Everyone seems to be sleepwalking this week. What do you think is going on?"
- "This month is crammed with 'must meet' deadlines. Can I bribe this group to include a few working lunches with some pizzas and Chinese food?"
- "These temporary digs are rather drab. Does anyone have a few posters or pictures that have been relegated to storage? They might work wonders here."
- "Some of us are sensitive to the new paint (or carpeting). Let's put up with a little cold air to clear out the fumes."
- "The fumes from the _____ (new paint job, new carpeting, renovations…) are pretty strong. We've rented an air purifier for the week."
- "Let's take a group coffee break. I ordered doughnuts and fruit. We can afford 20 minutes away from this."
- "Maybe completing all these projects as promised was an unrealistic goal. I think Client X has some leeway and might give us a few more days. Would that help?"
- "This has been a rough quarter, but we've got a lot of talent here. Let's focus on our past accomplishments

➡

and go forward to repeat them."

- "We are starting a new incentive program with great rewards for your hard work. Let's schedule a meeting early next week to kick off the new program."
- "We have so much to accomplish before the new store opening. I suggest everyone focus on key tasks. Worrying about how we'll get it all done depletes needed time and energy."
- "Losing customer X was a major setback. Let's examine why we did and discuss ways to make up the lost revenue."

Part Three

Motivational Rewards: Perfect Benefits, Perks, and Rewards

Beyond the energy, the kudos, the recognition, the support, *and* the paycheck are tangible (and sometimes intangible) rewards, perks, and benefits. Yes, most people work because they must earn a living. The fortunate work at jobs they love—or at least like—in environments that make going to work a positive experience. So, what else do they want? And what about those who are not tuned in or turned on by their jobs, those who view going to work as one notch above or below going to the dentist? What can make them want to give their all?

The number and types of benefits, perks, and rewards you can provide are all, of course, based on your organization's financial ability, corporate policy, and union agreements. No one can afford to provide all, but considering the full spectrum will help you choose which would be most valuable to your employees. When you factor in what you can afford, remember the costs of nonmotivated employees, especially when they leave and must be replaced. The effects of a motivated, dedicated workforce must be crunched into the hard number calculations.

Chapter 9

Perfect Benefits

"No one does anything from a single motive."

—Samuel Taylor Coleridge

The demand for new and changing skills, the perceived demise of loyalty on the part of employee and employer, the skyrocketing costs of healthcare, and the fear of cracks and leaks in once-secure nest eggs, have affected what attracts and keeps employees. Potential employees look at flexibility, family-friendly policies, and strong benefit packages when considering where to work. Employees look at practical financials as well as flexibility and appreciation when deciding where to stay.

Benefits are what an employer offers above and beyond the basics. Maria Bordas, general manager of strategic planning and policy for the Port Authority of New York and New Jersey's Aviation Department, is known among colleagues and employees for her favorite quote: "What I think and what I believe are of no consequence... What is of consequence is what I do." Think about what you do to show that you care.

The phrases that follow are the positives, the ones you can say when you are able to offer the proposed benefit; for phrases to use when you cannot offer the benefit, refer to the Chapter 8: "Raising Morale in Tough Times," in the section titled "Tough Economic Conditions."

Health Insurance

The Motivational Mindset

- With the high cost of health insurance, employees value good coverage and factor it in with earnings. Health insurance is a valuable benefit that shows employees you care about their well-being.
- Consider a variety of approaches before selecting a program for your company.
- Shop for the best deal on health insurance so that you can pass the savings on to your employees.
- Ensure that employees have all necessary information about options and providers. Give employees the direct contact information for your broker or insurance carrier.
- Many people don't bother to learn the requirements and regulations on their own and can be hurt financially in a health crisis by not following certain protocols. Ask your broker to provide free seminars to help employees become knowledgeable healthcare consumers and to fully understand their benefits.
- Alternative healthcare is becoming a mainstream demand. Be aware of options.
- Employees have diverse healthcare needs. One employee might choose a lower premium and higher deductible than another. A split plan allows employees to choose from different plans, even different companies.
- A cafeteria plan (also called a "flexible benefit plan" or a "Section 125 plan") allows each employee to select from a menu of coverage options. Someone may, for instance, choose health, life, and disability insurance but not dental, while another employee might choose only

➡

health and dental. Cafeteria plans offer a tax advantage as well.

■ Smaller companies may consider providing "Volunteer Plans" for insurance such as dental, life, or long-term disability to allow employees the *option* of buying in without the employer having to meet participation requirements.

Motivational Phrases

■ "You will find information about our health plan in this packet and on the website."

■ "Feel free to _____ (ask me, call Karen at extension 286, call the agent, whose number is on the front of your packet) if you have any questions."

■ "We're researching health insurance plans. What's most important to you? Low co-pay? Having a particular doctor in network? Preventative healthcare rider?"

■ "Our plan offers a low co-pay and a preventative healthcare rider. We've found that those are most important to the majority of our workforce."

■ "Let me (or my assistant) know what insurance companies your doctor works with so we can try to choose a plan that works for most. I'm sorry, I can't make any guarantees that we will succeed in pleasing everyone, but of course, we'll do our best."

■ "I'm sorry about your daughter's illness. Our plan manager is a stickler for following the rules. I want you to get all the help you need, so please follow the protocol."

■ "I realize that the referral process is frustrating, but that kind of plan allows us to pay a larger portion for all employees."

- "So many employees have requested alternative care coverage, dental coverage, PPO rather than HMO, that we are instituting a menu format for healthcare benefits. Please review all options and related co-pays carefully before selecting."
- "Rest assured that your medical information remains confidential."
- "Many employees are investigating assisted living for their parents. Our lunchtime lecture will address that topic."
- "Of course you're angry about having your emergency care payment denied. Call Marie in HR to help you through the process of resubmitting."
- "I encourage everyone to take advantage of the reduced-rate annual physical. That's a key reason we chose this provider."
- "Call the provider's customer service line to ask your questions about precertification. Yes, you will reach a person."
- "Please attend the seminar. If you understand how your health insurance works you will be able to take full advantage of its benefits."

The Motivational Mindset

- A healthy organization is made up of healthy people. Wellness programs will provide a healthier, more motivated workforce. Investigate and share the wealth of available information regarding money saved by companies whose programs have resulted in reduced illness and injury, lowering the bottom line of healthcare costs.

- Wellness program targets may include nutrition, weight loss, smoking cessation programs, exercise, and stress reduction.

- Onsite fitness centers, reimbursements for gym memberships, work/life balance programs, health and nutrition programs, ergonomic assessments, injury prevention programs, and educational materials are among the contributions companies can make to a wellness environment.

- Exercise programs can be tailored to work-specific areas that are at risk of strain from particular jobs. Whether sitting at a computer or doing heavy lifting, low back exercises might be a strong focus for a workout.

- Rewards or points may be given for achieving measurable results, winning contests, or simply for participating in programs. Participation rewards can be based on the honor system, having employees sign in on having participated, or can be substantiated by a third-party observer (health club employee or team coordinator).

- Some activities that may earn wellness points or bonuses include completing a health risk assessment, blood pressure checks, walking, running, biking, tennis, weight lifting; maintaining low medical claims or sick days; participating in weight loss or smoking cessation programs; competing in marathons; playing team sports; or attending wellness lectures.

- Rewards for following a wellness program or achieving wellness objectives may include a reduction in (or cutting out) healthcare co-pays, increasing employer payments for health insurance, or offering health insurance rebates. Other health-related rewards may include time off for well behavior or fitness-related rewards such as t-shirts, gym bags, relaxation CDs, exercise DVDs, videos, or gift certificates to sporting goods stores.

- Organizations are available to coordinate a comprehensive program.

- Points systems can be run a number of ways. One way is to allow employees to accumulate points that can be cashed in any time with the value of prizes increasing as new plateaus are reached.

- Another system would be to make a list of 10 criteria and reward employees who meet a specified number over a determined period of time. You can offer one reward for an employee who meets 5 out of 10 and a greater reward for employees who meet 6 out of 10 and so on.

Motivational Phrases

- "We are offering chair massages in the cafeteria this week."
- "A number of people have requested early morning Tai Chi classes. I'm pleased to announce that they will begin next month on Tuesdays at 7 a.m."

➡

- "Our insurance carrier offers reduced rates for nonsmokers. Anyone looking to save on your insurance contribution may want to attend our 'Smoke Free At Last' program."
- "Our entire department participated in the in-house weight loss program. We lost weight and gained energy. Congratulations everyone!"
- "Since you stopped smoking, your work is consistently accurate. Perhaps those frequent breaks broke your concentration. I know you stopped for your own reasons, but I appreciate the benefits to the department."
- "The breath work course will help reduce stress and improve overall health."
- "We can all use some stress reduction techniques. Please come to this week's seminar."
- "Please feel free to borrow from the fitness library."
- "We are all aware of the rising costs of healthcare. If you can help us and yourselves by participating in the new wellness program, we can help you with lower rates and co-pays."
- "We are offering one day off (or 1/2 day) to anyone who successfully completes one of our wellness programs."
- "The weight management meetings will now take place during work hours, from 1:00 p.m. to 1:30 p.m. on Mondays and Thursdays."
- "Human Resources e-mailed everyone an invitation to attend the presentation and kickoff of our new wellness program. We offer several ways to participate and a great rewards program. Please don't miss this opportunity to hear the coordinator's comprehensive overview."
- "Attendance at the nutrition web-inar will earn 10 points toward your wellness program goals."

Retirement Plans

The Motivational Mindset

■ Ask your broker to give a free seminar to educate employees about the plans and equity incentives you offer. The most effective plans will have little effect on motivation if employees don't fully understand the benefits.

■ A strong retirement plan attracts strong employees. The 401(k) plan (or 403(b) for nonprofit corporations or schools) provides a sense of security, which is a strong motivator for many.

■ The small business alternative to 401(k) plans is the Simple IRA. The Simple IRA allows employers to set up long-term savings plans for employees without high fees and overwhelming paperwork.

■ Corporate matching of 401(k) funds shows a strong interest in the individual employee's future well being.

■ 401(k) plans have tax advantages for both employer and employee. When considering a 401(k), evaluate cost, investment of time, setup effort, and investment options.

■ If your 401(k) allows employees to select investment options, educate employees about the risks and opportunities of investing. Keep employees informed about how their investments are doing.

■ If your company is publicly traded, stock options are an inexpensive way to offer a big payoff, create an employee-ownership culture, and encourage buy-in in the company's success.

■ Profit sharing plans give employees a sense of ownership, which adds greatly to incentive and to feeling like part of the larger picture.

- Educate employees on the market. Provide materials and links.
- Educate employees about retirement planning.

Motivational Phrases

- "Those of you under 40 may think it's too early to plan for retirement. The earlier you plan, the more financially comfortable and personally rewarding your retirement will be."
- "Our Succession Planning Program not only brings new talent up the ranks, but ensures that those who have contributed consistently to the organization leave well compensated."
- "For a small company, we offer a variety of options for retirement savings."
- "Every new employee orientation includes a segment on retirement planning options. Anyone can check the calendar and register for that component. We encourage that."
- "Because many people keep looking for a 'better way,' we regularly bring in speakers for a variety of investment areas—stocks, bonds, real estate investments—for our lunchtime learning series."
- "In today's economic climate, you can't just close your eyes and hope your money is 'working smart.' Either you watch it carefully or pay someone else to watch it."
- "We offer strong retirement incentives to continue to create room at the top."
- "There was some confusion about the 401(k) plan. These are your benefits and you have a right to understand them fully. If you have any questions about the plan,

➡

please see the 401(k) link from the website or call extension 201."

- "We are running a web-inar on retirement investing. Attendance is optional, but I hope everyone will attend and feel free to post questions."
- "Stock options are a way for you to invest in yourselves."
- "This is your choice and any stock, even one that we firmly believe in, is always a gamble."
- "We offer stock options because we want you to share in our success. We encourage you to follow the corporation's stock. It's your company, too."
- "Every day you're working toward our future. We'd like to help you work toward yours."

Personal Days, Sick Days, and Vacation Days

The Motivational Mindset

- Rather than the standard allotment of a number of vacation, sick, and personal days, each a separate category, many companies offer a package of days. This allows, appropriately, for the extended vacations or the unexpected personal event.

- A strict policy of a set number of days that expires annually forces employees to "use them up." Less rigid personal day policies benefit both employee and employer.

- Separating sick days, personal days, and vacation impedes flexibility.

- Packages allow employees with minimal health problems to be available for ailing parents or sick children. Packages simplify tracking and paperwork.

- Packages eliminate the employee's need to justify the time out.

- Allowing personal and vacation days to rollover from one year to the next is a small thing that can make a big difference for someone who would like to plan for an extended holiday or a reasonable length of time to visit distant relatives.

- Rollovers and packages work well for employees who would be penalized by losing days off when the year ends. Not everyone works the system.

- Rollover eliminates a sudden employee shortage during the month of December.

➡

Motivational Phrases

- "We offer personal day packages to give you the freedom to use your days whenever and however you'd like."
- "If you're planning to go to Europe again next year, you might want to save up some vacation days to allow you a longer stay."
- "We offer _____ days per year and they roll over for one year. These may be used for illness, personal days, and additional vacation time. Everyone's needs are different."
- "Congratulations on your excellent no absentee record. I'm sure those extra days will make your trip home more convenient."
- "We don't want to penalize employees for being healthy and dedicated. Our package plan works like a bank account with days in it ready to use when needed."
- "How exciting that your niece is getting married in India! I'm glad the package plan will give you the time you need."
- "What a shame that you had to cancel your December cruise plans. The good news is that your vacation time rolls over to next year."
- "You spent your day off working from home to help us out in a crunch. Of course, that doesn't count as a personal day. You get a do-over."

Flextime

The Motivational Mindset

- Flextime has become an important consideration for many in the workforce.
- Employees value—even demand—attention to work/life balance or, as it is now called, *work/life effectiveness*.
- Flextime attracts talented employees who might otherwise not be able to bring their skills and abilities to the workplace.
- Flextime reduces requests for time off and/or late arrivals/early departures to attend to family and personal matters that a nine-to-five schedule cannot accommodate.
- Employees who have the freedom of flexibility are willing to come through in a crunch. Many service jobs don't require a nine-to-five presence. Often, flexible employee hours benefit customers and clients as well as employees.
- Flextime does not mean a free-for-all.
- The more flexible you are, the more important structured scheduling becomes.
- Flextime provides for a routine that keeps work flowing smoothly.
- Don't arbitrarily suggest flextime when other solutions are more viable.
- Flextime can be a lifesaver for anyone with young children.

Motivational Phrases

- "Hit or miss scheduling doesn't work, but tell me which time frame is best and I'll try to work with you."
- "I realize that our eight-to-four schedule has been a problem for you. I appreciate your trying to make it work. What flextime hours would work best?"

➡

- "What would your ideal working hours be? Let's see how close we can come to that."
- "Would shifting your workday to start one hour earlier help you with your afternoon childcare issues?"
- "I don't want to lose you. Let's see what we can work out."
- "As long as the work gets done on time, it doesn't matter what time you're working on it."
- "I'm sorry I can't give you exactly what you're looking for in flextime. I wish I could. Would this alternative work for you?"
- "Congratulations on the adoption. I'm sure we can adjust your schedule for the next few weeks."
- "Flextime benefits all of us; however, the system works best when we establish a schedule and, barring emergencies, stick to it."
- "We all want to accommodate one another, but last-minute schedule changes disrupt workflow and productivity. Let's work out best times and stay with them."
- "Julio, your work is 95 percent communicating with clients by phone and PC. During your wife's recuperation period, I have no problem with your working from home."
- "Naomi, I understand that a full-time office schedule no longer works for you. Would you be interested in continuing to handle e-mail inquiries from home and coming in once a week to update us?"
- "The traffic from and to your area during a.m. and p.m. rush hours is horrendous. You can save at least one hour each way if you start at 10 a.m. and stay until 6 p.m. What do you think?"

"While your car is in the shop, you can have some latitude to conform with your temporary car pool."

Chapter 10

Perfect Perks and Rewards

"Nine-tenths of wisdom is appreciation."

—Dale Dauten

Our emphasis throughout this book has been motivation through communicating your expectations, satisfaction, and recommendations. Feedback—honest, timely, and concrete—motivates. Chapter 9 addresses tangible motivators and programs that show employees that you care about their health, well being, families, and futures. Chapter 10 goes to the next level: What more can you do to encourage and reward excellence? How can you spur, excite, and entice your employees to reach for the brass ring?

Denise Rounds, owner of Bellezza Salons at three Atlantic City casino/hotels—the Hilton, Caesar's, and Bally's Park Place—has developed a dedicated corps of full- and part-time workers. "I run contests regularly, always with an educational benefit. The winner of our recent hair color contest will travel to Italy with me—some education, mostly fun. Our staff takes great pride in the salons and their work. I encourage ownership, letting people make decisions about their customers, getting as much input as possible from the people who do the work."

The Motivational Mindset

- Not all public recognition requires formal awards and certificates. Public recognition can come in the form of announcements at company events, bulletin boards, press releases, company newsletters, and website.
- A certificate, plaque, or trophy is a lasting symbol of gratitude for excellence. Certificates are low-cost ways to show your appreciation or acknowledge accomplishments, but don't give them out so liberally that they lose meaning.
- If you or your department is the recipient of an honor or reward, share the limelight.
- Committee appointments within the company and without say that you have confidence that someone will represent you and your company well.
- Groom employees to present information, findings, or ideas at company meetings.
- Delegate key responsibilities that involve others— internally and externally.
- Pass customer/client letters of praise up the chain of command. Don't keep your shining stars under a cloud.
- Use your company website to acknowledge outstanding achievements.

Motivational Phrases

- "We present this customer service award to honor your customer care skills and the smile our customers mention on so many of our customer care surveys."
- "These certificates represent completion of _____ hours of training. This was no small achievement. You each

➡

worked hard and pulled through a tough course. Congratulations! You are now _____ (name, new title, or level of achievement)."

■ "Congratulations to _____! This month's customer service award goes to _____, for her ongoing commitment to customer care."

■ "As you know, I have received this year's outstanding manager's award. I share that honor with you. I know how lucky I am to have each and every one of my department members working with me. This award is for all of us. Congratulations to you, and thank you."

■ "The company has been named one of the top 10 in our industry. Each one of you contributes to that success and deserves to feel very proud. Thank you all."

■ "I received a letter from Customer X praising your handling of a difficult situation. I'm going to copy our VP with a note that this is typical of your work. You make us all look good."

■ "I've noticed how diplomatically you handle the turf skirmishes around here. The company is creating an Internal Public Relations Committee and I'd like to suggest that you be on it."

■ "Your ongoing research and recommendations for improving production have been outstanding. A Best Practices Committee is forming to study company-wide processes and related processes in similar companies. You would be an asset. May I submit your name?"

■ "I've been asked to represent the company on a statewide Supplier Diversity Council. I'd like you to attend with me and serve as my alternate."

■ "Our company website is starting a section, Kudos of the ➡

Month. I've submitted your recent turnaround project for inclusion."

- "Our department is responsible for the fiscal report at the quarterly meeting. I'd like you to work with me on my presentation and attend the next meeting with me. Eventually, I'd like you to take over."

- "When you draft the information for the press release about our company's participation in the charity event, remember to include your role. It was critical."

- "So many in our department have contributed creative ideas to the strategic planning process that we've been acknowledged in the company newsletter. Thank you all!"

- "So many customers comment regularly about how gracious and helpful you are that I've submitted your name and accomplishments for Employee of the Month. Good luck!"

Bonuses, Incentives, and Tuition Reimbursement

The Motivational Mindset

■ When people go above and beyond or their work on a particular job brings in a substantial amount of money for the company, share the wealth with a bonus.

■ Bonuses show appreciation, create a sense of buy-in to the company's success, and inspire higher levels of work and dedication in the future.

■ People expect holiday bonuses and those who say "bah humbug" will forever be known as Scrooge. Whatever your faith, whatever you feel personally about holidays, commercialization, or religion, you live and work in a culture where this is a time for giving. See what is reasonable within your budget and join in the joys of holiday giving.

■ While cash is a great motivator, products and experiences are long-lasting and long-remembered, making them more lasting ways of feeling the company's appreciation and generosity.

■ Companies specializing in incentive programs offer every solution from scratch-off cards with a variety of possible perks to comprehensive online points systems, including specialized catalogues and phone support.

■ A points system allows employees to enjoy immediate rewards or earn bigger rewards over time. You might let employees choose from among a variety of rewards: golf, hot air balloon ride, cruises, show tickets, restaurant gift certificates, spa packages, or gift cards from leading retailers.

- Computer-based incentive programs can track and record performance markers and points earned.
- Your company logo is not always appropriate on employee incentives and rewards. Items without logos may feel more like gifts and less like advertising.
- Encourage growth and foster skills that will allow you to promote from within the company. Tuition reimbursement may be applicable to college courses, degrees, external seminars, or online courses. Investing in employees promotes a high return on investment.

Motivational Phrases

- "Thank you for your hard work and dedication. Your input made the difference."
- "Because you went so far above and beyond the call of duty, you deserve to share in the wealth of this latest success. Thank you."
- "It was a great year! Thank you for all of your hard work."
- "Our company management wants everyone to understand the incentive program so you will be sure to enjoy the rewards. Human Resources e-mailed the promotions site and logon information to each of you with an explanation of ways to obtain points. I know we have a department of winners. I'd like you to be rewarded."
- "If you have any questions regarding the new incentive program, please call extension 208. I want everyone to understand the system so you will be able to enjoy the rewards of your hard work."
- "Congratulations, Jack! I signed onto the system and saw the number of points you've accumulated this month. Great work! Do you know what reward you'll choose?"

➡

- "Brian, you will receive a cash bonus at our customer care meeting this month. Customer comments, supervisor observations, and coworker comments show that your caring dedication keeps customers returning and makes coworkers appreciative."
- "Ricardo, your saving that contract that everyone else gave up on was masterful. You will find a well-earned bonus in your paycheck."
- "I'm delighted that you want to move up to a paralegal position. Of course, tuition reimbursement is available."
- "I understand that you're interested in earning a degree. Let's discuss what tuition reimbursement options are available to you."
- "We cannot provide full tuition reimbursement, but we can help you in other ways. For example, every employee has a maximum education allowance and we can work out flexible scheduling while you're in school."
- "While your support services are outstanding and I'd hate to lose you, your math skills make you a natural for the accounting department. Would you like to take some courses to build your confidence in that area?"
- "Having that degree would certainly put you in a better position for promotion and I believe you would be an asset at that level. Would you be interested in discussing a tuition reimbursement program?"

Contests and Competitions

The Motivational Mindset

- Contests may be centered around sales numbers, customer service ratings, or any other measurable result you want to inspire.
- Beware of running a contest that defeats its own purpose. A sales contest that inspires pushy tactics in an atmosphere where a soft sell is most appropriate may inspire your customers to go elsewhere.
- Contests and competitions, if promoted in good spirit, can be motivational, but do not promote a cutthroat atmosphere; ensure that everyone has a fair chance.
- Establish and reinforce customer care standards. Then reward those who surpass your benchmark.
- Stipulate how many times in a row or in a year one person can win contests. If one salesperson is more seasoned than the others and has a long-established client base, others may not even come close enough to feel motivated to strive.
- Let the top performer know your appreciation publicly and privately, but have an honest conversation about trying to motivate those who are struggling to make the numbers. You may find this top performer willing to let go of or divide the perk.
- If you have people working in two leagues of success, offer two rewards. Offer the "Grand Prize" and "First Place" or "Salesperson of the Month" and "Star Seller."
- Devise a system that works, keeping in mind that motivation is the goal.

➡

Motivational Phrases

- "This is a friendly competition. Let's maintain the supportive environment that I know this team creates."
- "Each month the winner will receive a gift certificate to dinner at Chez Shishi. Rules are posted on the board and on the website. Good luck!"
- "This year's winner will receive _____."
- "Monthly top performers will receive _____."
- "Contest winners will be posted on the board/website."
- "Dave and Hanna decided to remove themselves from the monthly competition to give our next generation of salespeople a chance. As you know, with their long histories here and well-established client cases, they have been our two consistent winners. In addition to monthly contests, the first person to break Dave or Hanna's numbers will win an additional prize." (name the prize)
- "This month, we are looking for the best team. Choose a partner for the month. Any support you can provide each other will strengthen your team."
- "The shift that gets the most positive customer comment cards this month earns 25 bonus dollars for each employee."
- "We know that customers are more outspoken about negative than positive events. The company created a simple one-minute feedback card to ensure that more employees get the praise they deserve."
- "Whoever can list the most names of our regular patrons will win our *We Care* Award this month."
- "In addition to exceptional service, we honor outstanding acts. This year's honoree is Ricky."
- "Our *Teacher of the Year* Award goes to Shu Chou,

➡

whose personal, caring approach has helped countless underachievers become successful college students."

- "Congratulations to Sashi, our Employee of the Month for the third time this year. Enjoy the day, Sashi."
- "Amos, you regularly win a Star Award for customer service. We're going to try something new—a partner award."

Gifts and Special Occasions

The Motivational Mindset

- After an especially taxing day, a small surprise waiting on the desk (even a candy bar or piece of fruit) in the morning with a note shows your appreciation. Any small, unexpected gift to say "Thanks" or "You're doing a great job!" can make someone's day.

- If you have a formal incentive program, do not give small gifts in lieu of points. Someone who is working toward a catalogue item will most likely wish you showed your gratitude in points (if it is up to your discretion).

- A hand-written note becomes even more caring as the custom fades.

- You might want to bring back a small gift from the islands for the person who picked up your slack or took care of a difficult problem while you were gone. Don't bring back gifts for some and not others with the exception of the person who took care of things for you when you were gone.

- If you choose to give a personal gift for birthdays or holidays (holiday gifts do not replace bonuses), choose something appropriate. A gag gift you would give to a friend might not be appropriate in the office. Giving a gift of a sexual nature constitutes sexual harassment.

- Birthdays are personal holidays and many companies include birthdays off in their packages. If you cannot give a birthday off, a lunchtime or short office celebration shows that you believe the person and the day are special.

- If someone is sensitive about a birthday, respect that person's wishes and privacy. You can still celebrate the ➡

people who enjoy it without making the ones who don't uncomfortable.

- Weddings, commitment ceremonies, births, and adoptions are important events and should be acknowledged and cheered. Depending on time, budget, policy, and often size of your staff, choose an appropriate level of celebration. Be sure to treat all like events the same.
- While acknowledging occasions makes people feel good and gives everyone a chance to celebrate, it's important not to burden people with gift-giving obligations, especially in a large department.

Motivational Phrases

- "Remember our policy of birthdays off. Put in for the day early and ensure coverage."
- "With our flexible scheduling it's hard to pull a group together for occasions. I'd like to take you out for a birthday lunch."
- "Go home a little early today and enjoy the rest of your birthday."
- "Let's take an afternoon break to celebrate Kim's engagement."
- "We all signed a card for Katelyn's birthday. Let's be sure to do the same for Larry's next week."
- At the end of an e-mail update, on a calendar or bulletin board: "Happy Birthday to Leona!"
- "You mentioned that you're sensitive about your birthday. We love to celebrate birthdays, but we don't want to make anyone uncomfortable. Are you okay with your birthday _____ (being announced, being celebrated over lunch, being celebrated on an afternoon break)?"

- "Congratulations on the adoption! I know how long you've been waiting. Several of us would like to celebrate with you over lunch."
- "I appreciate all the late nights you've put in lately. Enclosed is a gift certificate to the Brick Oven for you and your wife to make up for one of those dinners you missed at home. Enjoy!"
- "I found this beautiful handcrafted box on my vacation. I hope you like it. I was able to totally relax knowing you had things under control. Thank you."
- "I picked up a bag full of fun stuff from the trade show. Everyone, feel free to dig in and take something you like."
- "I won these specialty chocolates in a raffle. I'd like you to have them."
- "I hope these flowers brighten your morning. Thanks for working so late."
- "I know how you enjoy your mid-day chocolate charge. With all the pressure of the last few weeks, I thought you could use some Godiva. Enjoy it!"

Conclusion

We mentioned self-motivation in the beginning of this book and would like to close with a friendly reminder. Whether you are a supervisor or a business owner, it's a struggle to fire people up when your own fires are barely burning because of overwork, lack of sleep, or no time left in the day, week, or month to enjoy the rewards of your hard work. Many of the most put-upon employees are those who are *self*-employed or dynamic entrepreneurs.

As you focus on motivating employees, think, as well, about your own motivators. If you started this venture to afford a beautiful house you hardly see, a boat you never seem to get to, or vacations that your schedule won't allow, it may be time to think about your own perks and rewards. It's never easy finding time, but even small rewards keep us inspired: a hot bath at the end of a long day, quality family time, relaxing with friends, a weekend getaway without the laptop, or that class you've always wanted to take.

Airplane safety instructions tell us to put on our oxygen masks first so we can assist others. That theory helps with motivation, too. Be inspired and you cannot help but to inspire others.

About the Authors

Harriet Diamond recently sold Diamond Associates, Multi-Faceted Training and Consulting, a firm she created in 1985. She designed and delivered a full spectrum of programs and services that spanned all areas of oral and written communication, personal development, and management skills. Through those programs, she and her team have motivated and informed staff members, supervisors, and senior executives throughout a broad range of businesses and industries.

The author of six books, Harriet has addressed a variety of audiences on topics related to communication, management, and motivation and served as consultant to two work-related educational series. Her credits include a number of published magazine articles. She received three NJ Author's Awards and several honors, including The New Jersey Business Woman of the Year, Salute to Women Leaders Award, and a NJ Senate Citation for Outstanding Contributions to Adult Education. Harriet currently serves on the Advisory Board of *Enterprising Women*, a national magazine for established women business owners for which she writes regularly.

Linda Eve Diamond has been in the corporate training business for over a decade, writing, customizing, and designing training materials in all areas of communication. Additionally, she is a contributing author and editor to *Executive Writing*, *Writing the Easy Way*, and *Grammar in Plain English* and has written a number of technical manuals for several industries.

In addition to writing, Linda has been an adjunct professor of writing and reading at Middlesex County College in New Jersey. She has also given talks regarding her work in communication in her role as advisory board member for an organization that helps transition talented lower income teens into successful college careers.

Linda's writing and design of print materials for Diamond Associates earned her an award from the New Jersey Association for Lifelong Learning, and her poetry, which has been published in literary journals, won a small press award.

Currently, she serves on the board of the International Listening Association (ILA) for which she is the editor of *The Listening Post*, an ILA newsletter publication.

The authors, a mother-and-daughter team, have collaborated on several writing projects. The two have shared a uniquely strong working relationship either due to or in spite of their family bond.